VICAR Alan Bartlett

Celebrating the Renewal of Parish Ministry

First published in Great Britain in 2019

Society for Promoting Christian Knowledge
36 Causton Street
London SW1P 4ST
www.spck.org.uk

British Library Cataloguing-in-Publication Data
A catalogue record for this book is available from the British Library

ISBN 978-0-281-07917-9
eBook ISBN 978-0-281-07918-6

Typeset by Manila Typesetting Company
First printed in Great Britain by Ashford Colour Press
Subsequently digitally printed in Great Britain

eBook by Manila Typesetting Company

Produced on paper from sustainable forests

Contents

Contents

Part 3
WHAT SORTS OF PEOPLE ARE VICARS?

CONCLUSION

Preface

This book really matters to me.

I know that all books ought to matter to their authors but this one really does matter to me – because the future of the Church of England (hereafter C of E) is at stake.[1]

I have belonged to, and served in, the C of E almost continuously since I was about eight (as choirboy, lay member, youth worker, lay minister). I have been an ordained minister in the C of E since 1991 and have served continuously in parish ministry (nine years as an incumbent), including as a volunteer when my 'day job' was non-parochial. I have spent 12 years as a member of staff in a theological college and also working for the local non-residential theological training course, helping to prepare ordained ministers for the Church (Methodist and Roman Catholic as well as Anglican) and also running 'in-service training' for serving clergy and laity from almost all the denominations in England. I was recently moved to a diocesan post as Ministry Development Advisor, where I continue to support *all* our diocesan ministers, ordained and lay, parochial and non-parochial. All of these posts have been indescribably beautiful gifts.

But I am worried.

I am worried because, under the multiple pressures of secularization, financial problems and profound cultural change, the C of E is being stretched as it has never been stretched before. This is not to say that as an institution the Church in England has not endured aggressive external and internal pressure in previous eras. My first training was as a historian, and I know that we do not now have to dig up our saints to keep them safe from the Vikings (Cuthbert); or suffer multiple violent switchbacks of government policy as during the Long Reformation and Civil War, including the execution of an Archbishop of Canterbury; or struggle to cope with the previously unimaginable economic and social changes of the Industrial Revolution. We must not feel sorry for ourselves! And nor are we the first generation in the C of E to hear predictions of its demise. In the 1830s, Thomas Arnold thought that the C of E would not survive another generation: 'The church as it now stands, no human power can save.'[2] He has been proved wrong and I am confident that similar prophets of doom now will also be proved wrong.

But the C of E is being stretched. In too many areas we are struggling to fulfil, with any visible effectiveness, our commitment to provide a 'Christian presence in every community'. Stipendiary parish clergy are having to cover ever larger areas and more churches. Volunteer clergy are being used to plug gaps, without the cultural change in the local church that was always recognized as essential if that was to be life-giving let alone sustainable. Local congregations are often ageing and shrinking, and some lay members are having to take on significant leadership roles without adequate preparation. Some of all this is creative and vibrant. Much is long overdue. But within it is a growing unease. I hear vicar after vicar say, 'The Church no longer values my ministry' – good active priests as well as our worn-out, disillusioned, even broken priests. This feeling is prompted in part by the brutal facts about where the C of E is spending its money: new initiatives, not propping up failing parish ministry ('after 40 years of failure, we are no longer throwing good money after bad'[3]). And that is felt to reflect (inaccurately, I am sure) the current judgement of the senior leaders of the C of E, as opposed to the former commitment to the 'mixed economy'. But I have recently been working with a newly forming group of churches where the parochial stipendiary posts are being reduced at the same time as huge financial and human resource is promised for new missional activity – Resourcing Church – in the *same* group of churches. When the parish clergy and laity in this group wonder if the C of E still values parochial churches and their ministry, it is hard not to agree with the question – even if I and they are excited by the new possibilities.

The people at the sharp public end of all these 'stretchings' are the parish clergy, the vicars.

I believe in vicars. (Fundamentally, of course, I believe in the God who has provided this way of being actively present in our communities.) When I think back to those who have most inspired me, many, though not all, were vicars.[4] I can picture them still: leading our worship; teaching the faith with integrity; loving with a bloodhound-like tenacity; managing the mass of minutiae (with varying degrees of patience and success); and being known and trusted, and making a difference in our communities. Vicars and, symbiotically, the local churches where they belong and serve are a precious gift to our communities. It is a tragedy that they are being lost in so many places. I treasure Bishop Paul Butler's formulation of the C of E's current aims: we are committed to growing our churches, 'because growing churches are good for their communities'. They surely are, and are to be celebrated and encouraged, together with the vicars who lead them.

We will come to more bad news in a moment, but this book is about celebrating being a vicar. I hope it will be an encouragement to those who are called to this ministry, to those who pray and work alongside them, to those testing their call to this ministry, and to the opinion formers in the C of E who must make hard decisions about the best use of limited resources.

I am going to use the word 'vicaring' as shorthand for this role and work,[5] partly because whatever the C of E calls us officially (Rector or Team Rector, Vicar or Team Vicar, Parish Priest, Priest in Charge, Associate Priest or Minister, Interim Minister, House for Duty Priest, Local Ordained Minister, Pioneer Minister), our communities look to us as their 'vicar', the one who will, however inarticulately they may express it, 'do the God stuff for them' and care for them in Christ's name. If the people in 'my' parishes wanted to contact God, they knew where to come, and they still do. Commercial enterprises would give their back teeth for such clear brand recognition. Vicar: it is the word our communities have heard for centuries and it comes with a rich hinterland of associations, mostly good, though not always. And while it is different for colleagues in different denominations, in more ways than not, the work of vicaring is something all of us in local church leadership do. This book is written knowing that in every place where I worked I was working alongside ecumenical colleagues. This is *not* a book of English Anglican imperialism, though there is a particular responsibility on the C of E as the Established Church of the English State and people to be the public Church for England. This is partly what gives C of E vicaring its unique character.

So this book is really aimed at those who are exercising in effect a ministry of what the C of E calls incumbency, or aspiring to it, or thinking about it; being legally and spiritually in charge of a parish and the Anglican churches in it. This includes those who have a role as the visible local leader of a church community but without carrying the legal responsibilities of incumbency. And while pioneer ministers have a different role, as they lead and care for a local church, and as they function as a key interface between that and the surrounding communities, so they too are functioning as vicars. The more visible they and their church communities become, the more they will be seen as and function as vicars within their host communities.

Writing this book has felt more like walking along Striding Edge (a narrow ridge in the Lake District where the path clings to the top of the ridge with steep slopes on either side) than anything else I have written. The C of E needs its vicars to lead (we will return to feelings and reflections about the word 'leader' later in the book). Most dioceses now have leadership programmes designed to enable their incumbents to be more skilled and confident in leadership. This is a relatively new development. I am on the team in Durham Diocese that delivers our 'Missional Leadership for Growth' programme. But all the time we are also saying to each other as vicars that all leadership must be collaborative. In the era of *Setting God's People Free*,[6] we are requiring our vicar leaders to lead in a new, particular, highly skilled and self-aware way – collaboratively. As I will stress early on in this book, I do not want to be heard as taking sides in a crazy debate pitting clerical leadership against enabling the life and ministry of the whole people of God. Enabling leadership requires highly motivated leadership from vicars who are clear about their identity and role.

I must also note at this stage that I write as an Irish-born English Anglican vicar. I cannot comment at depth on how vicaring is done in other parts of the Anglican Communion or in other parts of the Church, though what I have seen and heard suggests some overlap. I also write as a man and am conscious that women may do vicaring differently.[7] This will emerge explicitly at different points in the book and, I fear, unconsciously when my prejudices will be evident to women colleagues. But this book is written from among and for the parish clergy of the C of E.

I know that vicaring needs renewing and reforming. This book is *not* an anachronistic plea for the 'good old days'. But I am sure that vicars (inseparable always from the local churches they help to lead) are good for our communities. I think vicars in their local churches are the best way for the C of E to fulfil its promise to provide a 'Christian presence in every community'. They help make Christ present everywhere. If we stop striving to make this a reality, then we will have stopped being the Church of England, which in God's providence has been given the task of being the undergirding Church for the English.

This is why this book matters to me.

And it is why I am so grateful to Bishop John Pritchard for encouraging me to write it, to SPCK and my editor Alison Barr for taking me on. I am also grateful to the diocese of Durham for space and time to read, think and write. I am especially grateful to dear and determined colleagues who have given up much time and energy in reading and questioning drafts. The book is hugely better for their help – the Revd Dr Richard Briggs, the Revd Canon Sophie Jelley, the Revd Sarah Lunn, the Revd Professor Walter Moberly and the Revd Dr Gavin Wakefield – but responsibility for the final text rests firmly with me.

Preface

There are many outstanding books on Anglican ministry for which I am very grateful and which discerning readers will see have shaped my own thinking, but this book is deliberately written from a personal perspective rather than as part of an academic discussion.[8] The endnotes are there to provide the occasional justification for the words in the text but much more to suggest further reading on key topics. In other words, the tone of this book is experiential rather than academic. It has grown out of my own experience of parochial ministry and much conversation with others.

The shape of the book is in three parts: Part 1 lays some theological foundations; Part 2 explores the practice of vicaring; Part 3 explores the qualities that are required of those who are vicars. Finally, I conclude with a theological reflection on 'success' in ministry.

Profound thanks must also go to the churches and communities on whom I practised vicaring: St James', Bermondsey; Holy Cross, Fenham; St Mary's, Throckley, and the other churches in Newburn Parish, Newcastle; St Margaret's, Durham; St Giles', Durham, and St Mary's in Sherburn and St Cuthbert's in Shadforth; and finally, St Edmund's in Bearpark.

The most important thanks must go to those who had to put up with living with a 'stretched' vicar: Helen, Ben and Annie.

Part 1

THEOLOGICAL FOUNDATIONS

1

Introduction

Vicaring

I love being a vicar. Personally speaking, I think it is the highest vocation for a priest in the C of E; though I honour deeply priests with other vocations, not least the chaplains who are often truly the front line of the Church.

Being a vicar is, as it has often been, an impossible role to fulfil adequately, and it is currently becoming more complex and challenging. But I love it: the sense of being part of a great adventure with Christ, trying to discern Christ at work and join in; to see the light go on in someone's eyes as they realize that Christ loves them. Before a recent school confirmation, we were having a practice with the children. After the bishop had explained what was going to happen, one of the children exclaimed: 'Does that mean that Jesus loves *me*?' 'Yes.' Job done, or at least started. Even after 26 years I still pinch myself at the humbling joy of helping to lead Christ's people in their praises and prayers, breaking open the word and sharing the bread of life, and knowing those with whom I do this, caring for them in their hurts and happinesses and watching 'my' people grow in faith, confidence and ministry. But for me the equally great privilege is to be with all sorts of people, whatever their relationship to the Church and at the profoundest moments of their lives, with Christ. To be known, trusted and loved as Christ's person in this place, in our community, is an immense privilege.

But I am deeply worried because what we have is not quite working.

Problems with vicaring

We cannot pay for the number of vicars that this traditional model of ministry requires. In many places our congregations are increasingly fragile and the whole system is creaking. Vicars are spread too thinly on the ground to exercise this personal ministry effectively. They are often overworked, and frankly too many are demoralized. But just for a moment it is worth noting that the problem is really the C of E's, in that we cannot sustain the system we created whereby people relate to God through their vicar and local visible church. If we think about the problem from that perspective, it makes the current crisis in the C of E look rather different.

I was on a training day for vicars in multi-church benefices. We were helpfully being introduced to new models of how churches might relate to each other – 'minster model' and 'satellite churches' or 'resource churches' and their neighbours – so that we could sustain our parish ministry. I summoned up my courage and said: 'But isn't the problem that our communities know how to contact the Church, and indeed God? They come to the church or the vicarage, or look for the website or find us from "A Church Near You" and then email; but they come looking for a person. And we are struggling to provide that person. Who is the identifiable "person" for them?' I expected to be howled down. But in fact the trainer (and the cluster of clergy) agreed and began to tell us about dioceses that are experimenting with training and resourcing self-supporting clergy with small groups of lay people, or groups of lay people, to be that 'person', the visible face of the C of E for that community, the 'vicar'. These initiatives are excellent, though rather overdue.

There is a deeper problem. I am worried that as the C of E transfers resources from nationally supported local parish ministry we are really saying that we are losing confidence in our local (parish) churches and in the work of vicaring that is inextricable from them. I trust this is not the case and that as an institution we still believe in a 'mixed economy' where 'doing traditional church well' sits alongside fresh expressions as a God-given and God-blessed task.[1] But I know that many parish clergy feel alienated from the current rhetoric of the C of E and are anxious because their skills and values do not seem to be valued or needed any more. The 'Experiences of Ministry' surveys that have fed into Ministry Division reports about Continuing Ministerial Development (CMD)[2] have identified that clergy see as their own values and self-description that they are people who pray and pastor – the 'pastoral paradigm' – whereas it is perceived that the C of E is requiring its vicars to be entrepreneurial, managerial and evangelistic, where many vicars feel least capable.

This is not, I hope, an anachronistic book. Our context has changed dramatically since the 1950s, let alone the 1550s. We cannot and should not just try nostalgically (using the word in a negative sense) to maintain a way of being the C of E that in so many ways was a Victorian creation, in that particular social and economic context. How local clergy have exercised their ministry has changed profoundly down the centuries and we need to recognize this so that we can be better equipped to make wise decisions about how it needs to evolve. For example, given that the large majority (over 70 per cent) of C of E vicars do their vicaring across two or more churches, how do we do this now? How do we translate the values of a George Herbert – of whom more later – about presence, visibility and pastoral care, into teamwork, intelligent working and right use of the ordained?

Times they are a changing . . .

We are living through at least two epochal changes. The first is the 'liberation of the laity'. Whatever the clergy used to say to themselves about being the only skilled Christian disciples in a locality, this is evidently not the case now. In the historical period that has seen the 'rediscovery of the laity'[3] – ecumenically, liturgically, ecclesiologically – how is vicaring to be done in this context of collaborative ministry? We appear not to know the answers to these questions yet, as is evident from the contested language about 'leadership' in the C of E, in the continuing grumbles among the laity, especially lay ministers, about clerical autocracy, and from the clergy about not quite knowing what they are for!

Reflecting on my reading about ministry in the Church, going back for almost forty years now, it feels like much of the new material was couched as an attack on traditional ways of being church and specifically on the role of the vicar within that. 'How can the Church have been so stupid as to believe it should be organized into one man/one church geographical areas?' Of course, that was a historically clumsy attack. There were good reasons for organizing a Church whose key task was to sanctify (convert) its huge acquired membership by having at least one disciplined element within it, the clergy. Deep development is needed, but it has too often been couched in denigrating terms for the inherited tradition – often from a position of ignorance about the Anglican way[4] – and has become linked to deconstruction of the role and value of ordained parochial ministry, vicars. So vicars feel threatened, are tongue-tied about their own vocation and lose their sense of purpose. Christ sent us prophets – Paul, Tiller, Greenwood[5] – to help us think about development, but we have not really heeded them until change is being forced on us. And I cannot say too strongly again that this book is not about taking one side in some crazy debate: should the Church put its resources into clergy development or lay training? It is a no-brainer. We have to do both simultaneously. But to make the C of E work we need a high and evolved theological understanding and practice of vicaring.

So, I confess that I am at heart a 'Gregorian'.[6] I believe that if the Church is to be renewed it will be because the clergy are renewed, and especially our incumbents. This is partly for pragmatic reasons. Incumbents are the gatekeepers and bottlenecks to renewal in the C of E. When renewal has been attempted in the C of E and the parochial clergy have been resistant, the result has been schism. Methodism is the clearest example; though I wonder if some of this lies behind the creation of the New Churches in our generation. But I also believe that renewing the parochial clergy is the priority because the C of E at the Reformation opted to remain within the broad tradition of Western Catholicism, with a threefold ordered ministry and a parochial structure. The vast majority of the C of E and of English people still live in this continuing mode of being church and so we need to make it work.

This is rightly having to change as we live through the second epochal change, what is called post-Christendom (though I think that is patchier than its proponents believe), but it is where we have to start. Across almost all of Western Europe, the Church has lost numbers, social significance and political and economic power since the middle of the seventeenth century. It is a peculiar and self-damaging imitation of alleged ostrich behaviour to ignore this. This has not been a continuous process – late-Victorian Britain was substantially more religious than mid-eighteenth-century Britain – and nor do I think it is an inevitable one. But the shift from a monochrome theocratic agricultural society to a pluralist, structurally secular and industrially postmodern society is a reality and it is folly to ignore this new context. It is arguably a unique context, in that the self-conscious dismantling of a religious state is a modern phenomenon.

Having said that, for those of us who have lived and ministered in working-class communities, 'liquid' does not adequately describe this world. And I am not convinced that the C of E should regard the shift to a more atomized 'global' economic and social order as either inevitable or self-evidently beneficial.[7]

Our context has changed massively, not least since the 1950s – the last 'Anglican decade'? Within this contextual change, the C of E also has to adapt, develop and regrow. From the Gregorian perspective, while the Church's ordained (ordered) ministers remain the bones that hold the Church together, as they have been for almost two thousand years, we now need growing, developing, hopeful, nurtured, living bones within more energetic and self-motivating bodies.

'Not true enough . . .'

We also need flexible bones – if that is not too nonsensical. The most chilling sentences I have read in recent years about the future of vicaring come from the pen of Jessica Martin. Jessica gave up (if that is the right word) a career as a Cambridge academic to become a vicar. She writes:

> I am personally convinced by the arguments for the English parochial system – convinced enough to have left another deeply rewarding vocation in order to serve it. I am convinced by its inclusive generosity, by its commitment to areas abandoned by most other forms of civic engagement, by the profound spiritual and practical possibilities of its civic and community role . . .
>
> I became a parish priest thinking that if one simply worked hard enough and with enough enthusiasm, if one were flexible and imaginative and generous and physically visible (it is an incarnational model), then the tradition would flourish . . .
>
> Perhaps I missed something obvious, but six years later I know that this is not true . . . well it's not true *enough*. Community goodwill is worth much, and we throw it away at our peril; but unceasing effort makes churches semi-viable without filling them . . .
>
> Even in the comparative comfort of my small group of commuter-belt parishes, no amount of energy, no amount of expended time or imagination, can make the Church thrive on the old model utterly unchanged.[8]

As I finish nine years as a Durham vicar, this is my experience also. It is '*not true enough*'. We have tried to be accessible, imaginative, outwardly focused in mission but the demographic is dispiriting (our older church members are disappearing at a faster rate than we can grow new ones). We are not yet very good at attracting new fellow disciples of Jesus. And the strain of the current workload is not sustainable. Change is essential. But I do not hear accounts of what this change will look like that quite convince me. Part of the purpose of this book is to explore possibilities for change that may be nearer 'enough'. To undergird that exploration, I will try to lay some theological foundations in these opening chapters.

I hope that by drawing explicitly on some 'Classic Anglican' sources (Cranmer, Hooker, Herbert),[9] the book will be able both to have some reflective Anglican depth as well as demonstrate the scale of the change. There is real treasure in our Anglican heritage, even if we must not in a fundamentalist way try to reproduce it now. I know that Herbert in particular has come to be seen as the bane of English Anglican parochial clergy, as his manual – *The Country Parson* (1652) – has allegedly got under our skin with its anachronistic and unrealistic vision of parish ministry.[10] But if we set up a dialogue with, say, Herbert's values rather than simply his practice, we will have a more life-giving conversation. What truths and values do we need to keep or reshape? As we do that historical theological work so we will be able to see more clearly where change needs to come. The Ordinals will also be an important conversation partner since they set the theological framework within which vicars operate. There is deep wisdom in how the Church has organized itself for centuries, and this book will try to have a conversation with that traditional wisdom in our new context.

My training has in part been as a practical theologian, so as well as weaving into the book my own experiences and observations from a quarter-century of ordained ministry, I will try to deepen them by use of practical theological methods.[11] In addition to stories there will be reflection on what is happening anthropologically, sociologically and psychologically, as well as theologically, in these events. Why do so many of the families who have suffered a suicide still bring their young men to our churches for their funerals? Why did the mum of one of these 18-year-olds ask to hold his funeral with us, even though she had become a member of one of the New Churches? Because this is the church her family have known – even distantly – for generations. Because this is where, she said, 'they will feel safe', even at this moment of heart-rending grief. Because, I think, she felt that vicars can be trusted to do this right. They are 'God's sensible people', not least because they wear archaic clothes! None of this was connected explicitly to her new-found faith in Jesus, but it is the context in which we live and the role that we embody. And in keeping with good practical theological method, there will be some practical ideas to take into ministry.

The Church and country still need vicars

Of the writing of books on ministry there is no end; inevitably, because our context changes and we need reflective material to be fresh and rooted. But what is the real justification for this book? The core message of the book is simple: vicars are still needed. As well as using some of our traditional language – priest, shepherd, parson – I will offer newer words to help us to reflect on this vocation: leaders, advocates, enablers, carers, functionaries (institutional servants) in the Church. And especially the old and new word 'example': vicars are exemplars of Christian living.

Vicars lead churches; collaboratively of course, always an enabling ministry, but we must stop being frightened of the word 'leader'. So I am using the word 'leader' deliberately because, while it grates on many of the parish clergy, in reality this is what incumbents need to be doing. I hope this book will contribute to drawing together the new language of leadership with some existing Anglican language of priesthood and especially vicaring. Advocates of the faith: this is a role vicars often struggle with but is now essential if the good news of Christ is to be spread again. Structurally, vicars remain as front-line functionaries of the Church. If we overlook our institutional role we are being naive and will become unnecessarily frustrated. Vicars are carers. It is the role in which we are most at home and, more importantly, it is the mode in which people expect us to operate. We ignore that reality at the risk of alienating our communities. And we are still examples, examples of what it is to be a public Christian disciple. In some ways I think this is the most important role we have, but we have lost sight of it in a false humility. It is weighty to be an example, but it is what we are, whether we like it or not, so we had better face the reality and pray for grace to live it as well as we can.

Using Avery Dulles' simple models of the Church as the backdrop,[12] I will argue that these descriptions of the role of vicars crucially are true both for the 'Church as community of the disciples of Jesus' and for the 'Church as institution'. One of the deep unacknowledged problems in the modern C of E is our struggle to hold together both the newer emphasis of being 'a community of disciples of Jesus' and also, still and for the good, being the 'Church as institution' for our country. As we will stress again and again in this book, vicars do not function as 'Church' single-handedly. While some ministry is solitary, all vicaring depends on the life and love of the local Christian community, especially the creation and nurture of new Christian disciples. To put it positively, 'Church as institution' is simply providing a structure and systems to join in with the work of God in our communities (the *missio Dei*) and being organized and visible in such a way that our communities can access us. Even given some reality behind the slogan 'the end of Christendom', culturally in much of England the C of E still has an institutional presence and will always be an institution.

It is also true that in many fundamentals the work of vicaring has not changed. The vicar still leads her people in their prayers and praises, cares for them in their sufferings, rejoices with them in their joys and does this both with those who 'come to church' and those who don't, and tries to point them to Christ, breaking and sharing word and bread of life. But how do we do this now in sharply changed circumstances without 'throwing the baby out with the bathwater'? What more is needed if it is to be 'enough'? If the Church is 'sign and instrument of the kingdom', then its vicars are 'sign and instrument of the Church' as 'sign and instrument of the kingdom'. But what are they to do and point to?

Or, to turn the question around, how do we re-evangelize England? How do we subvert secularization in its many guises? Our work as vicars in local churches is a crucial front in this struggle.

One of my fellow dog-walkers, a prison officer, fell into conversation with me one day. He asked if I had read the *Da Vinci Code*. I made some critical remark. (It is one of three books that I have thrown across the room!) He replied that he didn't believe it either. But then he said, 'It had never occurred to me that the Church might make up what is in the Bible.' He was not a churchgoer but was friendly to the Church. Reading this book had taken him over a new threshold of scepticism about the Church and about Christian faith. We should ask, 'How might he be helped to trust the Church again?' So it might be right over a cuppa or in a group to debunk this particular book or even give an account of how the canon of Scripture was agreed. But for any of *that* to be possible, there needs to be an emotional readiness to engage on the part of my fellow dog-walker. Such a person may now be sceptical about the Church, but if the vicar is compassionate, competent, clearly believes in God, does the christening/wedding/funeral well, or whatever is the point of contact, is humane and friendly, then my fellow dog-walker may be open to thinking again.

Evangelism by integrity and caring action and *then* word – this is the mode in which many English people are still able to receive an invitation to faith. English people expect their vicars to be pastoral. We know that we need to move on beyond that, but it is where we mostly need to start. I believe these are good tactics and part of a wider strategy of renewing the Church's – and, beyond this, Christ's – reputation.

Thus vicaring is hard and skilled work and it feels that it is increasingly so. Without colluding in clerical self-pity, this book, by celebrating and underpinning the work of vicaring will, I hope, be both a contribution to lifting the morale of the incumbents of the C of E and also to helping us to continue to adapt. The more the C of E asks of its vicars, the more we need clarity about this role and, even more deeply, a sense of its value if we are to sustain our priests in this ministry.

I remember a conversation with a senior incumbent of one of the great historic churches in the C of E, who had come to me to explore taking an MA as part of his CMD. He argued passionately for 'every-member ministry' and for a reduction in stipendiary ministers (vicars) because they were no longer needed. But as we explored the job he actually did, with all the challenges of helping to manage a major national heritage site, leading a complex team, being one of the key public representatives of this institution in a large city, and so on, it became evident to both of us that this was a demanding role that required not just a wide range of skills but deep personal capacity. His parish needed the best vicar it could get. For a liberated laity the Church needs valued and vibrant vicars.

Most deeply, I hope to hold up to myself and for others the simple reality that vicars need to strive for Jesus-likeness. Where the key cultural test is authenticity, we need to hold before ourselves the highest standards of spiritual life and ethical and emotional living. I use the word 'Jesus-likeness' deliberately to jar because it is awkward but also because it takes us back to the humanity of Jesus himself and a vision of what God incarnate is like. Values such as humility, accessibility and flexibility may need to renew older ones such as authority, reserve and faithfulness. I unashamedly believe that clergy should be held accountable to the highest standards. It has always been so in the C of E because the clergy represent the Church, and so Christ, publicly.

Keble, one of the founders of the Oxford Movement, who spent many years in parish ministry, once said, 'If the Church of England were to fail, it will still be found in my parish.'[13] We are not in this place – predictions of the demise of the C of E have occurred every century since it was reformed and none have been fulfilled. But Keble's angry and melancholic statement does reflect my own passions and worries. I think of the cities, towns and villages where I have served, especially our former pit villages. If the Church visibly withdraws from them, then we must be honest about the loss to these communities and to the life of God's kingdom. This is not to argue for trying to retain all the old structures, finances and services – or even all the old buildings – but it is to say that I think that the best way to share God's love with these communities is through a vibrant local church with a visible vicar. Commutable churches will attract the commuters from our villages, but that is not everyone who lives there. So how can we renew the role of the local (parish) church in the C of E and the work of the vicar within that? Because it really matters to the Church of and in England, and to England itself – it matters for the kingdom's sake.

And now for some theology.

2

Whose world is it anyway?

Why this question?

Whose world is this? We might think this is an obvious question with an obvious Christian answer – God's – but it is not quite so simple. However, a good and, from my perspective, Anglican answer to the question will provide the theological foundations for the work of vicaring.

Vicars have some clear ideas about this question. We see much goodness in 'the world'. As a parish priest I have seen extraordinary love as a family has cared for a dying member, nursing the person at home, sitting by the bedside for days so he or she is never left alone. I have seen the reality of community care, when hundreds turn out to show their solidarity with a grieving family and provide that network of support that enables a family to come through even the most heart-breaking of grief journeys. I have seen the dedication of teachers, health workers, social workers and carers, local authority staff, and especially volunteers, going the extra mile and far beyond. And I have found faith 'out there': the faith of a mother of a young man left paraplegic and bedridden after a car accident, who not only nursed him for three years as he slowly died, but prayed, evidently prayed. As far as I could ascertain, she had never been to any church, apart from 'hatching, matching and dispatching'.

Of course I have seen sin – indifference, hypocrisy, self-righteousness, as well as the consequences of 'sins of the flesh'. Sometimes the world seems a place devoid of any sense of God, or of order, meaning, compassion, grace. And part of the work of the Church – and its vicars – is to call out and work against evil in all its forms. So the priest is to 'resist evil, support the weak, defend the poor'.[1] But I believe that this is still fundamentally God's world, that God is still active in it and sometimes more evident in the world than in the Church – though I don't always live and minister as if I believe this.

We can put some theological flesh on these bones. If this world is not God's – if it is so fallen, sinful and rebellious that all those outside the Church are not just lost but are actually at war with God – then even if in the sovereignty of God this world will one day be redeemed, at the moment the world is not actually God's. It really is enemy territory, out of which the Church needs to rescue people and within which the most the Church can do is attempt to restrain evil.

This idea will probably come as a surprise to most contemporary English Anglicans, but the conviction that the world is so fallen as to be primarily under the judgement of God was a mainstream Christian belief. We could find it in John's ambivalent use of the word *kosmos*, where the world is both opposed to God (John 15.18–19) and also the object of God's love (John 3.16).[2] We could find it in Cyprian's slogan, 'there is no salvation outside the Church' – which fed into the mind of the Church of late antiquity and the medieval Church and has lingered.[3] We could find it in the Reformed doctrine of the total depravity of humankind.[4] For Anglicans, crucially, we could find it in the Book of Common Prayer where we pray in the confession, daily, in Morning and Evening Prayer, that 'there is no health in us'. We are simply 'miserable offenders' who have provoked God's 'just wrath and indignation against us' (Communion Service). This is described even more brutally in Article 9 of the Thirty-Nine Articles: 'Original Sin . . . is the fault and corruption of the Nature of every man . . . and therefore in every person born into this world, it deserveth God's wrath and damnation.' Thus the world is no longer really God's. The best we can say is that we can be saved out of the world into the 'ark of the Church'. So in 1549, Cranmer exhorted the soon-to-be-ordained priests 'to seek for Christ's sheep that be dispersed abroad, and for his children which be in the midst of this naughty world, to be saved through Christ for ever'.[5] A 'naughty world': this was a mainstream Christian belief and remains the view of some.[6] Indeed, priests are still to search for God's children 'in the wilderness of this world's temptations, and to guide them through its confusions' – even if this is not quite as gloomy a view of the world as in 1549.[7]

But the 'naughty world' was not to last as the mainstream Anglican view and it does not provide a good basis for vicaring. If we take Richard Hooker as an early and weighty touchstone of Anglican orthodoxy, then quite quickly this sense of the world as fundamentally and entirely a place of sinfulness and alienation from God was to change.

Note that Hooker also believed in sin. One of my reflections as I have come back to re-edit this text is that the stories we tell as vicars are so often stories of redemption, of love exercised in a hurting and damaged world. As I argue elsewhere, one of my favourite descriptions of God is as the life-giver, but this is in creation *and* redemption. The joy is that it is the same God who makes the sunset who comforts the hurting souls. The grief is that the God who makes the sunset has to take the cross into God's very being to transform the damage into resurrection.[8] It is in this tension between the fundamental goodness of this world and its extensive fallenness that the language of kingdom comes. The kingdom consists in glimpses of God's restored world, of the world a life-giving God makes and remakes.

Richard Hooker on God's world

The crucial foundation for Richard Hooker, and here he was building on Thomas Aquinas,[9] is that this is still structurally God's world. Hooker, unlike some of the other Reformers, retained a strong emphasis that this world is constituted by God and that this divine ordering remains effective. In other words, God has both created this world and embedded his laws (or, as we might say, 'principles') deep within it and they still have governing authority.

To go into more detail: Hooker argues that there are laws that flow from the very being and character of God-self: 'that order which God before all ages hath set down with himself, for himself to do all things by'.[10] Hooker names these as the 'eternal law'. We might say God's being is a law for his actions. God cannot be other than loving and just.

This 'eternal law' is then worked out in a series of other 'laws'. First, there is 'Nature's Law', which is the regularity by which the natural world lives. There is also 'Angelic Law', which is the law that all heavenly beings follow 'without any swerving', unlike human beings. Crucially, for our purposes and for Hooker himself, there was then 'the law of Reason'. This is the potential for rational creatures (human beings) to discern by reasoned thinking and discussion how this world works; God is to be seen in it as well as beyond it and also humankind can discern the values by which we ought to live. Hooker was clear that there were essential aspects of the faith that could only be known by special revelation – 'divine law'. His test case for this was belief in (the) resurrection, which he did not think rational human beings would discern simply by reason. Finally, there was 'human law', which is how humankind, provisionally, locally, imperfectly, tries to embody in codes of conduct and laws the application of all the above to a particular state or society or ecclesiastical institution.[11] So, in Hooker's world view, the laws even of human societies are connected 'upwards' to the eternal law in God-self. The principle of divine loving justice cascades down, however imperfectly, through the whole of creation. Further: *everything*, even when fallen and thus falling short of God's standards, is nonetheless still encompassed within the *ultimate* loving purposes of God, which are for the well-being of God's creation.

This Classic Anglican truly believed that this is still God's world. I wonder if this finds an echo in the sense of so many of our parishioners who understand what love is, have a sense of God and indeed enjoy the good things of God's world.

Richard Hooker on knowing God

Another way of thinking about this is to understand that God is revealed in life (natural and human) through human reason and through Scripture.[12] In other words, *there is not a rigid demarcation between the ways in which God reveals God-self.* Revelation in nature and in human society, both of which are accessible to obedient reason, would cohere with that of Scripture. Or to put it another way, it is the same God who creates and who redeems and therefore there are deep continuities between the truth revealed by reason and the truth revealed more directly by God.[13] Scripture points us clearly to faith in Christ, and this Christ is the *Logos* within and behind creation

(John 1.1–4 and Colossians 1.16–17). God's revelation of God-self to us in this world is all of a piece. This is why, I think, vicars keep bumping into God-ness and goodness in 'the world'. But it is also why a fundamental part of our role is to help people to see Christ within and through their world.

One of my seasonal baptism talks is in the style of panto – 'He's behind you!' Here are young couples, often with a deep sense of gratitude for this beautiful new life, whom they want to celebrate and share with family and friends, sacredly. There is nothing like a christening for saying that this baby is special *and* that we want her/him blessed by God. I have seen these same intuitions and emotions in the most faithful practising Christian families and in the most chaotic non-churched families. God-ness visible. The heart-breaking frustration for me as a vicar is that the deep meaning of these intuitions and emotions – God – is so much harder to articulate and make visible. So I say to the congregation: 'Look, there he is behind you. This great big God who loves you and is there for you!' Too often they look baffled and embarrassed.

This can also be put in terms of a classic Christian theological debate. With Aquinas, Hooker believed that grace perfects nature; it does not simply supplant it. In other words, there is not an absolute discontinuity between the 'before' and 'after' of salvation. We bring our natural human gifts – including for example, our reason, but also the need to live in community, to generate political systems, to learn by seeing and doing as well as by hearing – into the life of faith. Indeed, as Hooker argued extensively, we do and must bring our natural human gifts to the task of understanding and interpreting the faith. Nature and grace are inseparable. As Hooker, in one of his rare moments of explicit rage, exploded against the Puritans:

> You have already done your best to make a jar between
> nature and Scripture. Your next endeavour is to do the like
> between Scripture and Church. Your delight in conflicts
> doth make you dream of them where they are not.[14]

In other words, the damaging consequence of a theology that divides God in the world from God in the Church is self-righteousness, leading to arrogance, insensitivity and blockages to being the body of Christ in the world.

We need to go further, because Hooker had a third strand in his rope, as we have just read. We discern God in God's world. We hear God uniquely in the Scriptures. We are also guided by God through the Church, which, as the body that grows its Spirit-guided wisdom through time, we also call tradition. All of this can be condensed into the Classic Anglican methodology of Scripture, reason and tradition in trialogue as the best way of discerning the truth of God, not as separate or competing strands but precisely as a three-stranded cord with God pulling on all three together.[15]

All this is reinforced, with a clear and Hookerian stress on the primacy of Scripture within this trialogue, in the current 'Declaration of Assent' wherein the faith is '*revealed* in the Holy Scriptures', '*set forth* in the Catholic Creed' and that the Church is called upon to '*proclaim afresh* in each generation'.[16] We might translate this as Scripture, tradition and reason. And for the purposes of this book, we should also note the confidence of the Doctrine Commission and the General Synod that the 'historic formularies', (the Book of Common Prayer, the Ordinal and the Thirty-Nine Articles of Religion) of the C of E have 'borne witness' to this faith, as the Church has been led by the Holy Spirit. In other words, our historic Anglican documents are also a source of the knowledge of God – which is why we will pay attention to them in this book.

Meeting God in God's world

This confidence that this is still God's world and that the same God can be met in different elements within it has been brilliantly expounded by a modern Anglican theologian: 'Found Theology will argue that the perfection of God's revelation in Christ is not compromised by – indeed, precisely implies – an ongoing historical dynamic whereby in God, human beings are constantly invited to *relate the given to the found*.'[17] Here, a 'given' is one of the foundational documents (revelations) of the faith and the 'found' is the discovery of God's truth in the circumstances of life. As Quash puts it more colloquially, 'The God who has "stocked our backpack for the journey" . . . also "places things in our path", up ahead of us.'[18] And there is a mutuality between 'givens' and 'founds'. Both can illuminate the other. In other words, Anglicans need not be frightened of discovering new insights into God through encounter in the world and can be confident that their fundamental Christian convictions will really illuminate their life journey.

I remember shocking a young ordinand when I said that what had most changed my theology was pastoral experience. He had to cling on to the wall to stop himself falling down in shock and fear. For him, theology was all about a 'given' to which we had to conform. I suspect that God has fewer rules than the Church.

As a young curate, I was perplexed that we could bless second marriages but not conduct them. People would come straight from the Registry Office to church, in all their wedding finery, to have their marriage blessed. I believe Scripture gives us a true metaphor when it describes marriage as two people becoming one flesh. As a parish priest conducting many funerals, I have seen again and again the unique grief of one half of a couple when the other dies after decades of marriage. It is the pain of a limb wrenched off. The wound will heal over but the missing limb is not replaced. And of course this grief is felt by churchgoer and non-churchgoer. Marriage is a 'creation ordinance', not restricted only to Christians. Anglicans know this and so we speak softly about distinctively 'Christian marriage' and welcome all-comers. So, I believe in 'one flesh'. But I have also seen marriages that have died, or been murdered, or need a mercy-killing, where the flesh is poisoned. The metaphor is not a master. (Biblical scholarship has demonstrated the developing and complex theology of marriage in the Scriptures.) So it was with huge relief that I found myself as a vicar able to conduct, after scrutiny, second marriages. Of course it would be simpler to have a black and white rule. I suspect I have had the wool pulled over my eyes by some of those who came seeking second marriage, but I would rather live with the mess and risk than see people hurt, punished perhaps for their choice of life partner who has already been divorced. So the C of E changed its mind and amended its discipline as a result of honest biblical study, realization of the complexity of the tradition, and the wisdom of pastoral experience. And people were enabled to experience new life in God. We were catching up with God in God's world.

God in God's world – but what role for God's Church?

So this is still God's world. Another important Anglican insight flowing from all of this is that God's activity is not limited to the Church. There is of course a long-standing idea that there is an important distinction to be made between the visible and the invisible Church. Rooted partly in predestinarian ideas (God chooses who will be saved, but we as church don't always know who this is) and partly in the experience of serious sin among Christians, the idea had grown – much strengthened during the Reformation – that the true Church was 'invisible', known only to God, but that in the world Christians lived in, a visible but imperfect Church. This is part of the title deeds of Anglicanism. Article 19 reminds us that the Anglican Reformers believed that all the great ancient Churches had fallen into error, doctrinal and moral, and Cranmer's essay 'Concerning the Service of the Church', printed as a preface to the 1549 Book of Common Prayer, breathes a mood of weary realism about human institutions: 'There was never any thing by the wit of man so well devised, or so sure established, which in continuance of time hath not been corrupted . . .'[19] Even the C of E!

Hooker extrapolated this conviction radically. He too believed in the fallibility of the visible Church, so he argued that because the visible Church is fallen, and indeed fractured, it is not a certain guide to the will of God. So, to take an extreme example, we cannot be certain that even those whom the Church has excommunicated have been excommunicated by God.[20] Only God knows the secrets of the human heart. Therefore, there are proper limits on the authority of the visible Church. Anglicans believe in a 'modest' Church, not because they are 'wet' but because they properly limit its authority.[21] The visible Church and God's will are never to be simplistically equated.

Later theologians pushed the doctrine of the 'modesty of the Church' further. Is the Church synonymous with the kingdom of God? In some periods, this has been the view of the Church; that the kingdom of God is to be found *only* in the Church. But a rereading of the Scriptures, not least by the liberation theologians, revealed the 'unchurchyness' of, say, the prophets or indeed of Jesus himself. Their ambition is human flourishing in just communities. This reality extends far beyond the boundaries of the institutional Church. It is worth spending a moment to ask, 'How churchy are the Beatitudes?'

This could be heard as a lessening of the commitment to 'conversion'. If our goal is the 'common good', then what is the place of individual conversion in that strategy? Often it feels slightly underwhelming. What value one individual saved when our ambition is to see a whole generation housed properly?

As I will argue later, I do not denigrate the importance of spiritual rebirth, though I do want to assert that conversion is always for a purpose – liberation for service – not just as an end in itself. But I still do not have a neat solution to the issue of individual conversion over against social justice. This feels to me like a constant tension.

As a young youth worker in inner London in the 1980s, my neat and tidy doctrine of conversion was not sustainable in the face of the deprivation and profound injustice of what we saw and experienced. Individual conversion was not enough. Confronting racism was, certainly, about praying for individuals to be transformed. It was also about standing alongside those who were being persecuted and saying, 'This is not okay with God' and campaigning for good ways of living together. I was hugely helped by the theology and passion of other Christian youth-worker theologians, like Jim Punton of Frontier Youth Trust. As he said of his own similar experience:

This [working in New York] was a 'radicalizing' experience. I found my thinking on socio-political issues totally inadequate to the situation, but my understanding of the Gospel was also inadequate. What did the Lordship of Jesus mean in a ghetto area experiencing such powerlessness and deprivation?[22]

This was how Jim addressed the tension between conversion and social action:

There have been those who have seen mission simply as the changing of social structures, and have ignored the predicament inherent in Man himself: there have been others who have interpreted mission as the rescuing of individuals from society and are unaware of any concern of God for the community of Man. Both views are inadequate and unbiblical. There is only one gospel: it raises personal issues demanding personal change; it raises social issues demanding social change.[23]

Jim wore himself out teaching about and living for the coming of the kingdom, 'kingdom theology'. It set me on fire too.

We were having a discussion one evening in our Bermondsey youth group about what difference being a Christian made. Frankly, mine and some of my fellow students' contributions were a bit esoteric. Then one of our local young people said, 'Well, I don't jump over the ticket barriers any more. I pay for my underground tickets.' Real individual change. And ironically there is now an underground station in Bermondsey, which had been a very neglected part of London in the 1980s. Real social change. Both important, but not to be simply equated.

Individual renewal. Social justice. God wants it all. That young man went on to be a youth worker and prison chaplain.

The kingdom of God

God is growing God's kingdom: people and places where God's values are lived out and all that distorts creation and limits human flourishing is overcome. I know that I am at my happiest and healthiest when I have a big vision of God and the *missio Dei*. Many years ago I tried to put into words what I thought God was up to:

> So what is all this for? Crudely put, why does God make Christians? Indeed more profoundly, why does God make human beings? I don't want to fall into too facile a caricature, but in some parts of the Church, it can feel as if the whole point of being a Christian is to make other people Christians – a gigantic spiritual version of pyramid selling. The richness and breadth of the Christian faith compressed into repetitive hackneyed evangelism: 'Ten thousand thousand are their texts, but all their sermons one.' But if we were to go back to Irenaeus again, 'the glory of God is a human being fully alive', then we would give a bigger answer. God is most profoundly committed to human flourishing in this life as well as in the next. God is always the life-bringer.[24]

To be technical for a moment: we are justified by faith so that we can be sanctified; we are redeemed not just from but for; we are converted *to* Christ not primarily from something else; we are 'born again' to live.[25] It is not a soft option, this holistic kingdom theology. As Christians, as vicars, it demands everything from us and offers everything to us. It is a vision of life in all its fullness, beyond ecclesiastical boundaries.

If this is true of individuals it is equally true of the Church. A recent Roman Catholic textbook on missiology puts this very directly:

> One of the most important things Christians need to know about the church is that *the church* is not of ultimate significance To say this is not to deny the church's divine origin or to believe one whit less that it is 'the people made one with the unity of the Father, Son and Holy Spirit' (*Lumen Gentium* 4) . . .
>
> Nevertheless the point of the church is not the church itself . . . The point of the church is rather to point beyond itself . . . So completely does the church live for God's reign that, when finally it is fully established, the church will be subsumed into its all-encompassing reality. 'Only the Kingdom . . . is absolute . . .' (*Evangelii Nuntiandi* 8).[26]

So what do I think I am trying to do as a vicar, as a member and leader of local churches deeply involved in our communities? When I devote hours of time to helping our local church school to flourish – and our state schools too – is this a good use of my time? What does God's kingdom look like? Does it look like a community of children (surrounded by their wider families), being educated to be fully human – caring and self-aware, inquisitive, creative, able to read and count of course – and all in a safe spiritual context? I think it does.

When I was a theological college tutor we instigated a 'Schools Week', during which the ordinands were sent out to local schools of all kinds, to experience the challenges and achievements of school life. 'Schools Week' fell towards the end of the academic year. I remember clearly the grumpiness with which the ordinands faced this new initiative. I remember even more vividly the quiet faces when they came back a few days later. One posh young ordinand who had been particularly vocal in his grumbling spent three days in a Sunderland primary school. He said movingly on his return: 'That school is an oasis for those children.' In a disadvantaged community, with many stressed families, the school was a place of compassion, order and security. That is a glimpse of the kingdom of God.

Fellow travellers

As I write that, I have tears in my eyes as I picture the children coming to our local schools and what they received there. Such goodness. And then I find myself asking if I really believe in the *missio Dei*. Thanks to the paradigm-shifting work of David Bosch,[27] we have all learned that God's mission is huge; nothing less than the flourishing of the whole of creation and humankind as the pinnacle. And that God is active all of the time, mysteriously and collaboratively blessing creation. But my default mode is often to assume that we (the Church) have to do the actual work, alone. A youth project is needed. So the Church sets it up, on its own. There is concern about high unemployment and its corresponding social problems. We look on, feeling overwhelmed and defeated. But what is God doing about that, and with and through others?

The phrase 'fellow travellers' has odd resonances because of its roots in political communism, but as a vicar I was surrounded by 'fellow travellers' who were also committed to seeing our communities flourish. Some would name God. Others would name God differently. Some were searching. Some would not talk of God at all. But we were all pulling on the same rope. All were a gift and while I think it is presumptuous to call them 'anonymous Christians' (Rahner), they were caught up in this mysterious and collaborative *missio Dei*. As I look back, I wish I had been able to make more of those relationships. Collaborative working engendered goodwill towards the Church. And it brought the opportunity for blessing.

One of our former pit villages had commissioned a new marching banner. We were privileged to be invited to its unveiling. I was asked to bless it; a priest of the C of E being asked to bless a miners' banner, with so much bad history behind us (the Church profited from the labours and suffering of the mining communities). So why was *the vicar* asked to bless it? Because the vicar and the local church were trusted and had been committed to the community for years. In that moment, the Church – here through its public vicar – becomes a *sign* of the kingdom, of God's presence in the work of building community.

A key role of the priest-vicar is to be a watchman/woman.[28] This is of course not a role just for the vicar. Fellow members of the Church will often be involved in our communities personally and sometimes professionally. They often see things that the vicar doesn't. But at the very least vicars are required in their job description to be see-ers. Where can we see signs of the kingdom in our communities? Where is God at work? How might we know? And how do we join in? Because this is still God's world and God is still active in it.

3

What on earth is the Church for?

What is the Church for?

This is a composite story . . .

Grandma came to book the christening. Went in the parish diary. All very straightforward. When the time came to contact the family to go through the service and confirm the details, we couldn't get a response. In the end I popped round to the house. Still no response. So I wrote a little note and dropped it in. Grandma then arrived at the vicarage door. 'Yes, please can it still go ahead.' A little more conversation and the story came out. Her daughter, the mam, was on drugs and not always 'with it' and the dad is not on the scene. Grandma was struggling to care for her daughter and to keep the grandchild in the family. Brave and solid, like lots of our local grandmas. But no wonder contact is difficult: never a landline, and mobile phones come and go. So the service is held. Small congregation, unglamorous. Not the big wedding-style christenings as on other Sundays. And I could feel myself praying passionately for God's protection and deliverance for this little child as we worked through the liturgy. 'May almighty God deliver you from the powers of darkness . . .' I have a lump in my throat for most of the service. I know God heard our prayers. Grandma then brings the bairn to the parents and toddlers group. In a couple of years the child arrives in the church school nursery. At least the child now has some invaluable security and the grandma some equally invaluable support. Mam is probably beyond our expertise. But there is some hope here.

What other institution in our communities will do all this? Bless, pray, provide practical and emotional support, be a gate-keeper to other saving resources? None. Only the Church and, as the oil in the cogs of this institution, the professional priest, the vicar. Not the only person by any means. There are baptism vergers, parents and toddlers group leaders (also professional) and volunteers, church administrators (also professional); and then there are the other partners – social workers, health visitors, nursery staff, teachers – and the huge number of folk who stand behind all of this, supporting the institutions, but never quite knowing what is being done with their help. But we still need a vicar at the heart of it.

What is the Church for? As Hooker might have said, lack of attention to the foundational questions often means we begin our conversation on the wobbly roof of the church, wondering how we got here. There are many ways of addressing the question of the Church but as a vicar I want to say two simple things.

The first is that *Church matters*. However modest a view of the authority and sanctity of the Church is proper for Anglicans, it remains an essential part of Anglican soteriology – how humankind is drawn to God. If we had asked Cranmer where someone was most likely to encounter God, he would have pointed us to the public reading of Scripture in the context of communal prayer.[1] Communal worship remains at the core of Anglican identity. It is where we are formed in relation to God and each other; where we are spiritually fed in word and sacrament; and where we witness publicly to our identity.

It is why parish clergy still agonize over the loss of thriving Sunday congregations. It is more than the numbers game. It is where we show that we are alive in God. It is also the place – and it is often a specific building for English Anglicans – where God's grace is administered in the sacrament of baptism and in the sacramental actions of marriage and funeral rites. And because we are self-consciously part of the ancient catholic Church, we do all this in an ordered manner (with continuity to ancient deep liturgical patterns, the creeds and lectionaries – mostly). Public Church matters to Anglicans and when we lose confidence in the value of public Church, we soon become emaciated.

But what sort of Church? Here I want to go back to a standard text that offers simple models of the Church, but which has helped me to understand something of the current crisis in English Anglicanism. One of the models of church offered by Avery Dulles in his textbook *Models of the Church* is 'Church as institution'.[2] It is, unsurprisingly, normally the least popular model of the Church among ordinands. This partly reflects the unpopularity of institutions, the lack of glamour of the phrase compared to its competitors, and some lack of experience about the actual life and work of the parish churches and clergy of the C of E. Conversely, I find myself more content now to see the Church as institution.

This is partly because of the realization that we are an institution. If we are to understand ourselves as real church as opposed to imagined church, then we need to start by reflecting on our actual identity.[3] As a vicar I was institutionally provided, institutionally governed (lightly), but with a strong institutional role in our communities. I, and our congregations and church buildings, are here to do the God stuff publicly and, dare I say it, institutionally. We are the 'C of E' on the end of a phone when a funeral director wants to book a particular kind of funeral for the deceased and his or her family and friends. We are still the institution many people come to if they want their child to have the best start in life by being christened. They come to us because that is what they think we are supposed to do. And this is what our Church thinks (mostly) we are here to do. Notice, I am not debating the rights and wrongs of all this, simply and briefly describing what happens. And for centuries this is what the Church in England and the Church of England has done. Literally, in my former context, with a 900-year-old parish church. It has not always done this perfectly, or in the same way – or indeed even done it at all when the institution of the C of E has been over-stretched or weakened or corrupted. But as a vicar I am an institutional doorway into the grace of God. The task is not how to subvert this role but how to do it Christianly.

But the C of E has been, since the nineteenth century, a particular sort of institution. Much though we may curse the Victorians for constructing too many wobbly buildings, they created the C of E as we see and experience it.[4] It has relied upon: historic wealth slowly redistributed to undergird its national ministry; broad enough levels of support allied to wealthy benefactors to build and (less effectively) sustain parish churches; a model of discipleship that, for 'centre-ground' Anglicans for example, prioritized Christian living in family, neighbourhood and workplace over against extensive church involvement or even intensive expressions of the faith.[5] (This is not to say that the rather weak patterns of discipleship that are prevalent in areas of the modern C of E are in direct historical continuity with nineteenth-century patterns. The Victorians were often much more passionate about faith than we give them credit for, and this is true of much of the C of E well into the 1950s, as exemplified in the life of the new Anglican churches on the new housing estates.)

The essential fact is that in living memory, for many of our communities, the C of E has been a provided institutional presence. We know that the spiritual, economic and social fabric that undergirded this institutional presence is rapidly eroding. This has prompted the churches to develop new models of church life.

It is striking that between the first and second editions of *Models of the Church*, Dulles introduced a further model, 'community of disciples'.[6] This was picking up on the teaching of John Paul II but is part of a very widespread movement. Institutionally, the C of E (and sister churches) needs a different pattern of discipleship to survive. It needs its members to be more committed: more self-aware and articulate about the faith; more intense in their engagement in church life; more generous with time and money. Whatever some of the subterranean grumbles in the C of E about the growing dominance of a particular tradition, spirituality and style of discipleship, it is hard to argue with its brutal necessity. Our congregations are becoming – and may become even more clearly – 'committed communities of disciples'.

But if the C of E parish system is to work, there has to be an openness to God at work in our communities beyond the visible Church and a modesty about the authority of the visible Church.

Why vicars?

This development need not, but has, contributed to the crisis among the parish clergy. If ministry can be done by any or everyone, then what need of a vicar, especially an expensive and institutionally provided one? But the second simple thing to say about the Church is that *it has priests, vicars, and they are crucial*. Why? Why does the C of E ordain people? Set them apart by training, ritual, prayer and (mostly) uniform?

Cranmer believed in ordination. There are many detailed arguments that could be used to support this assertion,[7] but the Preface to the 1550 Ordinal is the clearest: 'It is evident unto all men diligently reading holy Scripture and ancient Authors, that from the Apostles' time there have been these Orders of Ministers in Christ's Church; Bishops, Priests, and Deacons.'[8] Except it wasn't 'evident'; and not just to the Anabaptists but also to (most) Lutherans and the Reformed. By 1550, the Anabaptists had been and partly gone from their Radical Reformation without priests but with 'prophets'. Luther, with his pragmatic church order, was already dead and Calvin had already reformed Geneva with four different types of ordained and lay minister, which included, crucially, no bishops. So we must note that Cranmer and his fellow Anglican Reformers self-consciously kept not just the process of ordination but also the threefold order of the primitive Church and, indeed, some of the specific elements of the medieval rite, for example the words used at the moment of the ordination of priests.[9] Cranmer's priests (the word 'presbyter' does not feature in the sixteenth-century ordination rites) continued to be the order in the Church whose sole responsibility it was to bless and absolve and preside at Holy Communion, alongside the renewed emphasis on preaching and teaching the gospel. A reader of Cranmer's draft 1553 Canons for the Reformed Church of England is left in no doubt that clergy were both to govern the Church and were under a stricter discipline than the laity.[10] The 'priesthood of all believers' is not a Classic Anglican doctrine.

Hooker is if anything even clearer than Cranmer on the distinctiveness of the ordained ministry, though he often echoes Cranmer's own words closely. Read Hooker's descriptions of the source and authority of the ordained:

> For in that they are Christ's ambassadors and his labourers, who should give them their commission but he whose most inward affairs they manage? What angel in Heaven could have said to man as our Lord did unto Peter, 'Feed my sheep: Preach: Baptize: Do this in remembrance of me: Whose sins ye retain they are retained: and their offences in heaven pardoned whose faults you shall on earth forgive.'[11]

> The power of the ministry of God translateth out of darkness into glory, it raiseth . . . men from the earth and bringeth God himself down from heaven, by blessing visible elements it maketh them invisible grace, it giveth daily the Holy Ghost, it hath power to dispose of that flesh which was given for the life of the world and that blood which was poured out to redeem souls.'[12]

> Whether we preach, pray, baptize, communicate, condemn, give absolution, or whatsoever, as disposer's of God's mysteries, our words, judgments, acts and deeds, are not ours but the Holy Ghost's.[13]

The ordained are Christ's own ministers. They have a more important ministry than the angels. They are 'disposers of God's mysteries' – and it is a long and weighty list. These words may sound uncomfortable for modern Anglicans with our proper stress on the ministry of the whole people of God. Why did Hooker believe and write this? He was, of course, a man of his age and these views were the norm in the sixteenth-century Church of England as they had been in the Church since the second century at least. The clergy did church. The laity (mostly) had church done to them. But what do we make of his views? Is it possible to reflect and even celebrate the weighty vocation of the ordained without automatically being heard as clericalist and hostile to the priesthood of the whole people of God? Or indeed as advocating a clerical caste, who are in some way separate from the normal rules of society, which was of course precisely the medieval system? (There lies some of the poison that has erupted as abuse in the Church.) I hope so. That old way of a separate caste is gone. We need to find new ways of understanding and describing the nature and role of the ordained.

But Hooker is, to my ears, even more shocking on the nature of ordination, unashamedly using the medieval language of 'character':

the same power is in such not amiss both termed a kind of mark or character and acknowledged to be indelible. Ministerial power is a mark of separation, because it severeth them that have it from other men and maketh them a special order consecrated unto the service of the Most High in things wherewith other may not meddle. Their difference therefore from other men is in that they are a distinct order.[14]

They which have once received this power may not think to put it off and on like a cloak as the weather serveth,

to take it reject and resume it as oft as themselves list . . .
but let them know which put their hands unto this
plough, that once consecrated unto God they are made
his peculiar inheritance for ever . . . voluntarily it is not in
the power of man to separate and pull asunder what God
by his authority coupleth.[15]

The indelibility of orders: whatever modern English Anglican
canon law might say,[16] these words are not often spoken out
loud now. Should they be left in the sixteenth century, with
other old conceptions of the nature of ordination – and the
authority of vicars?

I am not sure they should be consigned to Anglican anti-
quarianism, for theological and practical reasons. In the early
1990s there was pressure for lay Eucharistic presidency. The
House of Bishops commissioned some historical and theological research, which formed the basis for the 1997 publica-
tion *Eucharistic Presidency.* The report argued that the Church
has always protected the most important of its public actions
by carefully managing the people involved. So, specifically regarding the president at the Eucharist:

The wisdom of the Church over the centuries has been
that the celebration of this holy feast should be prepared
for with care. An aspect of that is the way in which its
presidents are chosen, then trained, and then constantly
nourished and supported in the life of priesthood.[17]

The report was careful not to claim a simplistic origin for precisely this discipline in the New Testament, but it did note that
the New Testament included many examples of authorization

being given to individuals to lead the Church and to exercise particular gifts within in it, and under a specific discipline because of their role (1 Timothy 3); and that the C of E was committed to the post-biblical but authoritative threefold order.[18] The report also argued in technical ecclesiological terms in favour of ordered presidency:

> the Eucharistic president is to be a sign and focus of the unity, holiness, catholicity and apostolicity of the Church, and the one who has primary responsibility for ensuring that the Church's four marks are expressed, actualised and made visible in the Eucharistic celebration.[19]

But it most connected with me personally when it described the experience of presiding at the Eucharist: 'It is this sense of the presence of Christ in his Church that the presidency of the ordained gives.'[20]

I feel closest to Christ when I am presiding at the Eucharist and sharing the bread and wine, especially on Maundy Thursday evening. It is partly the privilege of repeating the words of institution. It is also passing the bread to the communicants. As a vicar I knew almost all of the stories behind those bowed heads and outstretched hands. Joy. Much sorrow. Faith and need. I cannot feed and sustain them but Christ does; through these words, actions and bits of his creation, broken bread and poured wine.

This is a role I learned under my training incumbent, alongside my priest colleagues, and it is a privilege I share with my colleagues now. That the disciplined and ordered leaders and pastors of the local church lead the celebration of Christ's presence in the Eucharist (Holy Communion, Mass, Lord's

Supper) seems to me both right and inescapable. Pastors lead, care and feed spiritually. In fact they do this whatever label or uniform they wear, Protestant and Catholic. It is the nature and the heart of pastoral ministry. There is deep theological, historical and practical wisdom behind this practice. And in an era when the practice and foundations of priesthood are being stretched, even shaken, we can say that this is bedrock.

I do not find the language of 'ontology' helpful when I consider this reality. I think it belongs to a previous philosophical era. But I am touched by the language of 'character', allowing for us to move it from its more technical medieval sense to one more inclusive of modern conceptions of virtue. And when we weave this into the rich modern Anglican language of the priest as 'representing, focusing, and collecting, recognizing, coordinating and distributing the ministry of others', the ministry of the priesthood of the corporate body of Christ,[21] then we are on solid theological ground.

There is a further obvious point to be made. Cranmer and Hooker believed, and the C of E still believes, that God calls people into this ministry. It was part of the Book of Common Prayer ordination rite.

Do you think in your heart that you be truly called, according to the will of our Lord Jesus Christ, and the order of this Church of England, to the Order and Ministry of Priesthood?
Answer. I think it.[22]

And as was typical of Cranmer, slightly differently asked of deacons:

Do you trust that you are inwardly moved by the Holy Ghost to take upon you this office and ministration, to serve God, for the promoting of his glory, and edifying of his people?

Answer. I trust so.[23]

Hooker has a typical Hookerian section arguing with his Puritan opponents about the use of the phrase 'Receive the Holy Ghost' in the ordination services. The Puritans argued, rather literalistically, that it was not down to the Church to give the Holy Spirit. Hooker, of course, took them back to the words of Christ in John 20. He made a proper distinction between Christ and the Church. So the Church did not literally imitate Christ by breathing on its ordinands as Christ had breathed on the disciples. Nonetheless, he argued that this was the Church praying for the bestowal of the Spirit on this specific group of people at this specific moment in time: 'Whereas now, forasmuch as the Holy Ghost which our Saviour in his first ordinations gave doth no less concur with spiritual vocations throughout all Ages . . .'[24] Why have we rather lightly taken to giving such light weight to these centuries of practice and experience – in a most un-Hookerian and un-Anglican way?

This should not be taken as arguing against any development. As we have noted, Hooker was not naive about the disparities between sixteenth-century orders and passages of the New Testament. So he argued, for example, that apostles were equivalent to bishops, but prophets were lay and evangelists were senior presbyters who could be entrusted with missionary work, leaving the parochial clergy as pastors and teachers.[25] He also noted that Elizabethan deacons did more than Patristic deacons but regarded this as a legitimate development.[26]

If there is an area for development in the contemporary C of E then I suspect it is in the area of the omnicompetent vicar. While vicars, like GPs, are by virtue of their role generalists, the temptation on both their own part and that of their congregations to expect them to be 'good at everything' is simply fantastical and does not chime well with what we discover about the clergy when we conduct personality and vocation tests with them.

So to sum up at this stage, our historical theology and contemporary liturgy would suggest that priest-vicars have a particular vocation to represent Christ publicly and institutionally, especially in what we might call the most explicitly 'spiritual' actions of the Church, its worship, teaching and sacraments, as well as in what we might call the Church's external relations. This rather old-fashioned perspective may be surprising but it is within this that we will discover the roots for the re-blossoming of our vicars.

If you are a vicar reading this, can I ask you a question? At the annual parochial church meeting (APCM), do you say 'thank you' to the different officers and volunteers in the church? I know that some vicars make a point of not saying 'thank you', partly because of the real risk of offence if they miss someone out and partly because it is not their job to say 'thank you'. But who else is going to say it? And it needs saying. The first time I said a series of thank yous in one APCM, I reduced an 80-year-old doorkeeper to tears because he had not been thanked before. And I have struggled to get the words right when I say it. 'I am not saying thank you from me as vicar, because you are not "my" helpers – though I am very grateful – but this is a "thank you" from the Church.' Clumsy. It gets worse. At my last APCM, struggling to get the words right, I blurted out: 'Christ thanks you for what you do for his Church.' Better than thanking people for helping me, but a bit presumptuous of me to speak on Christ's behalf! On reflection, I realized I did that almost every day of the week – speak Christ's words. What a gift and responsibility.

So the vicar is at the institutional and personal face and heart of the local body of Christ. Note 'at', not 'the'. We will confront later the demons of clericalism. The vicar is not the sole face and heart of the local body of Christ but we are a particular expression of this heart and face, which is both institutional – we are often the public face and heart of the Church – and also personal. We are often the public face of the Church, those of us with dog collars on, and especially the vicars.

I remember as a curate, when there had been a local scandal of a priest convicted of child sexual abuse, walking nervously out of the parsonage wearing my dog collar. I am sure now it was mostly my imagination, but I felt people staring at me. 'Is he one of them?' It is why the scandal of clerical sin is so serious. When the heart and face of the body of Christ is wicked – not simply fallen – then Christ is dishonoured. But it was me wearing that dog collar in that pit village. I felt it.

In a previous parish I had been asked to organize some safeguarding training for our many children and youth volunteers. The team coming to do the training asked if they could bring a survivor. I naively said 'yes'. The woman who shared her story of childhood sexual abuse by her father told us that the first person to whom she had disclosed was her local vicar, who told her: 'Don't worry. He will grow out of it.' I felt as if my dog collar had been plugged into the mains electricity. It burned around my neck. I remember nothing else of the training. I remember the shame.

The following morning, in one of the mysterious little providences of God, I was presiding at the early Eucharist. As I broke the bread and poured the wine, I was still picturing the violated body and spilt blood. But somehow – and this is *not* about 'making it better' – together I, we, offered her horrible ordeal and my own much, much lesser embarrassment on the altar of Christ's broken and risen body. That felt like a profoundly priestly moment. And a little bit of the kingdom had shown through. The Church needs its priest vicars.

A personal postscript

I would not have ordained me! Thankfully, with hindsight, the wisdom of the diocesan director of ordinands, the bishop's advisors, theological college staff, training incumbent and above all the bishop prevailed, and I was ordained. I remember floating out of Hexham Abbey a foot off the ground, I was so full of joy – and relief. And then came priesting. As the bishop read the charge to priest/presbyters, all I could feel was this weight on my neck and shoulders. The responsibilities felt crushing. But I settled happily into priestly parochial ministry and let the memory fade. My second curacy coincided with the 'Toronto Blessing' and as a staff team we attended one of the renewal meetings. When it came to a time for discernment and prayer, we were invited to move around the room by our Anglican priest leader. 'If your hands are tingling, then please go to that corner because God may be calling you to a ministry of healing. If you can't stand still because your feet are tingling, then please go to that corner because God may be calling you to a ministry as an evangelist.' There were more examples given of spiritual-physical manifestations and I was beginning to suffer from an attack of scepticism. But then the leader said: 'And if you are feeling a weight around your shoulders, a yoke, then come to the front, because God may be calling you to a ministry of leadership in the Church.' I was rigid with bafflement. This has been exactly my experience during ordination as a priest. I do not ask you to put any weight on this anecdote, but it reinforced for me the reality of my own calling as a priest.

4

The mysteries of place

Stability?

When I look down the lists of vicars in our parishes, I am struck by their lengthy ministry in one place. Once upon a time, it was not uncommon for vicars to stay in one parish for more than thirty years.[1] These men gave themselves to one community for the best years of their working lives. And often not glamorous communities. Pit villages were vibrant self-sufficient places but until the creation of the National Coal Board with its higher wages and more secure employment, and the building of the new council housing estates, they were often poor, characterized by irregular employment and frequent mining accidents, inadequate housing and so early mortality of both sexes, and with social problems which we do not view now through sepia nostalgia. This was hard and normally solitary ordained ministry in what was not always fruitful soil.[2]

Thirty years ago I was part of the movement that mocked the sheer stupidity of the Church in ever thinking that one man and a church building constituted the mission of the Church in a place. Clearly it was a flawed model and indeed an increasingly outdated one, but now I reflect that I was not alert to the quiet spiritual courage of my predecessors. I find myself moved by their example. I cannot imagine giving myself in this way to a church and a community. Modern vicars tend to move every decade or so, even though the accepted wisdom on that is changing. (Bishop Paul Butler at a recent Durham clergy training day remarked that because of the complexity of incumbencies now, in particular the complex geography of multi-church benefices, we should be encouraging incumbents to stay for longer, not least because it takes longer to know and be known. This is exactly my experience.) This lifetime's service, articulated in the old language of a 'living' (another word for benefice), reflects an incarnational theology. The vicar, while parachuted in from outside the community, was supposed to give himself to the community as Christ gave himself to humankind, becoming one with us and living as a shepherd of his flock. As with the historical reality of mining communities, so with historical vicars, we do not look back to them through rose-tinted glasses. In our pit villages and in the south-east London riverside community of Bermondsey where I worked previously, the vicar lived in one of the biggest houses and in the nineteenth century would be one of the few people in a poor parish to have a servant. The incarnational principle did not often mean sharing in the lifestyle of his neighbours. In Bermondsey and in County Durham, oral history reveals an anxiety about the vicar as 'big man' whose shepherding authority was sometimes used oppressively. But the vicar – for good or ill – was a fixed visible point in what is now remembered as a stable community, a good place.

I have noticed how I have changed the way in which I introduce myself. Apart from 'Alan', thankfully – or 'Revd Alan' in school – on public occasions I moved from saying that I am the 'Vicar of St Giles' or 'the senior priest at St Cuthbert's or St Mary's', to saying, 'Hello, I'm the Vicar of Gilesgate'. I hope this is not offensive to my ecumenical colleagues, but it reflected an inner journey of feeling now both that some of my best love went out to the wider community, that it wasn't just limited to one of the churches where I was based, and, more hesitantly, that after nine years and countless public occasions and occasional offices I had become known and trusted by many there: I was now their 'vicar'. Of course, my responsibility had always been the 'cure of souls' of these parishes, and one of the deep joys of Anglican parochial ministry is that we are constantly reminded of our wider responsibilities; but I felt that I had become the 'Vicar of Gilesgate' and in a little way felt that I had earned it.[3]

Vicars are always vicars of somewhere. Sometimes the somewhere is not very well defined, or there might be too many somewheres for it to feel anything more than overwhelming, or indeed the somewhere might be a church with a city-wide ministry; but vicars are always vicars of somewhere. We are supposed to be part of the scenery. Is this anything more than a nostalgic walk-on role in some Agatha Christie thriller? Do we really belong to a 'place', and should we?

Changing place

The postmodern English Anglican Church faces an apparently more complex sense of place. I say apparently because the new towns and cities of the Industrial Revolution were much more chaotic and rapidly changing than almost anything we see in Britain today. The C of E really only began to cope institutionally once these communities started to settle in the later nineteenth century. Social fluidity is not as entirely new a situation for the C of E as some might think. But what does the 'incarnational principle' look like now when we might be ministering in a place with a rapidly changing population who relate more to their friends through social media than to their neighbours, and whose family (if they are still in touch) may live hundreds of miles away? I am constantly struck that for my own children, their closest relationships are with a network of family and friends scattered over the planet – though I also notice a strong instinct for sustaining deep face-to-face relationships. But here in our pit villages are people who still have four generations of their family living within yards of each other, most of whom will also be part of this online networked world.

Geographers, sociologists, anthropologists and theologians have given much attention to the question of 'place' and I find their ideas resonate with some of my intuitions and experiences as a vicar.[4] One of the most useful of the insights from these studies is the distinction between 'space', which we might describe as a geographical area but to which people have not given a meaning, and 'place', which is, to put it crudely, 'space with a meaning', or indeed 'meanings', as Philip Sheldrake would strongly remind us.[5] Place is a geographical area that for historical, economic, cultural and social reasons has been given a particular identity by its inhabitants.

It is striking that the Mission-Shaped Church movement justified so many of its recommendations on the basis of the work of social analysts, for example the sociologist and social theorist Zygmunt Bauman. So we create Liquid Church[6] because we think ourselves to be living in a 'liquid age'.[7] 'Place' is becoming a more fluid reality. Critics of the Mission-Shaped Church movement must face the depth and seriousness of the case made that in postmodernity, society has changed fundamentally. But I think it is a complex and varied process.

A recent book has offered us a different but suggestive slogan for understanding varieties of people, *The Road to Somewhere* by David Goodhart. Like much semi-populist analysis, the book needs to be read with discrimination, but Goodhart's categorizing of people as 'Somewheres', who have a strong sense of belonging to a particular place, community or family, contrasted with 'Anywheres', who sit much lighter to a local or even a regional identity, made some sense in my previous patch. Goodhart goes on to identify the former with more conservative social attitudes, particularly people who now perceive their world to be substantially one of loss – of community, identity, cohesion, value, virtue and money – whereas the latter are positive about the benefits of liberalization and globalization, the freedom to choose one's own identity, and prize autonomy above all. In the context of debate about the future of the Church's mission, it is striking that Goodhart calculates that half of the population are 'Somewheres' ('Anywheres' are 20–25 per cent), and even more striking that he cites statistical evidence that 60 per cent of British people still live within twenty miles of where they lived when they were 14.[8] Perhaps we are less 'liquid' than we thought, and if 'Generation Z' really proves to be more conservative (at least in some ways) than their predecessors,[9] then I wonder if we may need to be think carefully about how we balance the competing claims of resourcing the parochial church over against new forms of church. How do we decide which sort of 'place' matters most?

Of course, like most stipendiary clergy, I am an 'Anywhere' who has given himself for a time to being a 'Somewhere'. How does that affect *my* thinking and feeling?

There is a further unique complexity about 'place' for vicars. In our suburban Newcastle parish, it dawned on me that I was one of the very few people who lived and worked in the same place. During the day, the only people 'at home' were the retired, the carers for young children, those suffering from some social disadvantage and some bleary-eyed shift workers. Conversely, almost all of my fellow professionals commuted into our parish. Parish clergy are in an unusual position in that we straddle these divides. Along with the postal staff and perhaps some police officers, health workers or educational professionals, as parish clergy we know our patch better than anyone. Which streets are changing? Where are the pockets of poverty or social disorder? Where are the new developments and how are the people there relating to the rest of the existing local communities? Good parish clergy know the answers to these questions.

I wrote the first draft of this chapter at the end of an afternoon out doing 'follow-up' visits to christenings, weddings and funerals. As I walked and drove down the streets, it struck me how many front doors I knew and the stories behind them. This feels for me to be a hugely valuable part of parochial ministry, ministry to a community in a 'place'. I think of a recent big public funeral. There was the public ministry involved in conducting this complex funeral well, with respect and compassion, but later being trusted to be invited in to chat in the kitchen with the family trying to cope after this difficult bereavement (especially when they tell me that no other agency has been to see them at home). This sort of ministry slowly but steadily spreads a good reputation for the Church in a 'place'.

So good parish clergy know their patch and are known. Or rather, that might be so. I write conscious that in my former post I was incumbent for a very varied section of Durham City, ranging from expensive old and new-build housing for professionals, through extensive student accommodation to some of the poorest housing in County Durham, as well as a large 1960s middle-class housing estate. I could travel from *Coronation*

Street to *Brookside* just by turning a corner. And in our four villages, we had the core of the old mining communities, symbolized by the Aged Mineworkers' Association bungalows, alongside social housing of every decade, 1960s suburbia and the newest housing estates. As the incumbent there, I personally could not be present to all of these communities, adequately. Those days are long gone – if they ever existed everywhere. Vicars need new ways of helping the Church to be present.

But looking at these different houses only tells half the story of the complexity of 'place'. I can see Goodhart's divides in our communities. There are highly educated mobile students, especially postgraduates, who move in and out of our communities, for whom Durham is a beautiful and well-resourced place to live and study, mostly for just a few years. Contrast them with the adult children, whose fathers worked in the local mines and who are themselves steeped in the language and traditions of County Durham, but who work in a wide variety of occupations now. The divides are not neat and tidy. Why did the postgrads come to our 'bog standard' parish church rather than the cathedral or one of the big student churches? At one point we had six doctoral students in our congregation. It is in part because they were looking for a sense of belonging, of community, which is not just mobile and academically elite. And the children of miners are as likely to be found living in the middle-class estates as in the social housing. We can see social change before our very eyes. Retired miner after retired miner has told me how he did not want his sons to go down the pits. Now his attitudes and their attitudes can be hugely varied. They might be self-improvers and/or socialists – or stuck in a cycle of deskilled under-employment. And what of those who through illness, misfortune or poor choices find themselves stuck on the poor estates with few prospects (my former patch has some of the lowest educational attainment)? What does their anger or despair or nostalgia mean? Nor can we forget those with some get-up-and-go who got-up-and-left in the 1990s; the population of County Durham fell in that decade. Are such migrants now 'Somewheres' or 'Anywheres'? Especially when they come back 'home'? All this complexity about 'place' within a few square miles of the North-East.

So we must ask again: for English Anglican vicars and their churches, who pride themselves on being incarnated, what is it to live the 'incarnational principle' in such areas? What does it mean to be a 'Christian presence in every community' when 'community' can be so varied?

It cannot mean simply being territorial. Parishes are often artificial constructions that might or might not relate to the human geographical realities. Boundaries that made sense in the 1800s (or indeed didn't, like many Victorian lines on a map in Africa) often make no sense now. What does a parish boundary mean when it runs down the middle of a street and then through someone's back garden, as it did in one of my parishes? And even before that, in the North, parishes were often large because of the nature of northern geography (poor farmland and so scattered housing) or humanly impossible to work because they had been swamped by population growth. Leeds is often given as the textbook example of where the C of E failed in the early nineteenth century to cope with rapid urbanization and ended up (allegedly) with one church for tens of thousands. But Durham diocese in the first half of the nineteenth century, when it covered the whole of the North-East from Tees to Tweed, had only 80 parishes. No wonder there was space for people to disappear from church connection completely. Conversely, just two generations ago, Wickham pioneered the Industrial Mission because workers related to their geographical home patch in one way, but to each other and wider society in another way when in their workplace – and related to church very differently in each of those places.[10] Naive nostalgia for the parish is of no help to us.

But I am with Andrew Rumsey in thinking that the C of E has a particular vocation to take locality seriously. In a very evocative phrase, he writes: 'Jesus Christ is not only the clue to history . . . he is also the clue to geography.'[11] So he argues that the implication of 'The Lord is here' is that, just as Jesus Christ was fully incarnate in one time and place, so each place now finds its meaning as it is reorientated to Christ who is in, and is Lord of, this place too. In cruder hands this might have become a polemic 'for the parish', but it does not. When reflecting on fresh expressions and mission-shaped church, Rumsey argues: 'If social space, like skin, is constantly renewing itself, then it is essential that the Church's spatial praxis is intelligible in the contemporary situation – enabling the recognition of "Christ in our place" wherever that place happens to be.'[12] And these 'places' will be varied, as they have often been in history, and the Church has worked with them in different ways. Therefore vicars and local churches must now work appropriately in their unique 'place'.

Building place

Perhaps we should turn the question around. Instead of asking how vicars and local churches implement the 'incarnational principle' by immersing themselves in some community or network, should we ask how vicars and local churches help to build community, healthy human relationship, even (especially) if it is fragile to begin with? And is this a proper part of their role anyway?

To answer the second question first: yes![13] There are many ways to explore this but we will again take an explicitly English Anglican journey. How did Thomas Cranmer handle the issue of place and building good community? Cranmer may well have believed in predestination.[14] When pushed to its logical extreme, which Cranmer and his fellow Anglican reformers did *not* do,[15] it leaves an uncertain percentage of the population, the 'reprobate', hopelessly damned. This at the very least was likely to trigger moral and social disorder, so there was wise pragmatism in not announcing that predestination is true. But Cranmer went further. In the invitation to the confession, he holds this vision of the Christian life before us:

> Ye that do truly and earnestly repent you of your sins, and be in love and charity with your neighbours, and intend to lead a new life, following the commandments of God and walking from henceforth in his holy ways.[16]

The purpose of the forgiven life is to live as a good neighbour (as well as get to heaven!). The proof of regeneration is the reality of living in good relationship. We know that Cranmer, of all the Protestant Reformers, placed the greatest emphasis on good works – good neighbourliness – as the proof and out-working of salvation. So after communion we pray that we 'may do all such good works as Thou hast prepared for us to walk in', 'loving our neighbour as ourselves'.

If we follow Cranmer's teaching, vicars and local churches will find themselves actively and extensively involved in building community, facilitating good human relationships and directly loving those who are in need. I think of local church social events. Some slide into becoming cliques, but others are gatherings where lonely people find friendship, where people who don't cook for themselves get nourishing food, where there is laughter and light. The Church has no monopoly on such gatherings – though in my experience they can be very well done by churches – but I am struck by how many church members are involved, still, in non-church community-building events. I am told that the best pensioners' lunch club in County Durham is run in a local community centre by two church members. This building of community is more than a smart evangelistic ploy; we do it because it is good for its own sake. And we are respected because our communities know that we do this for the 'common good'. So what can be atomized space – loneliness is one of the most pressing problems in our communities – becomes a place where people move into relationship, build trust and find support.

John Inge describes 'place' as a humanizing reality.[17] After some time as a clerical nomad, and now being a little older and wiser, I wonder if a sense of belonging to a 'place' (even if we know that ultimately we are passing through – Hebrews 13.14: 'here we have no lasting city') is more life-giving and fully human than mobility. Rumsey asks a sharp question: 'Is it more Christian to be rooted rather than mobile in spatial terms?' He does not ask this question stupidly. We are aware that sometimes mobility is forced on people and also that mobility can mean freedom. But he makes a deep theological point: 'Settlement, then, is a spiritual issue – and for Christian neighbourhood to extend further than a kind of social first aid, it has to "take place" in shared space over time. *Every Good Samaritan lives somewhere.*'[18]

I have watched short-term Christian activism on poor housing estates. It is not without benefit but it so easily slips into patronizing do-goodery. If we are to be trusted, then we have to get stuck in. That takes time. It means being incarnated.

'Faithful capital'

The pit villages are changing. The collieries have closed, some only 25 years ago. Others closed decades before that as the seams were worked out. All of our pit villages have new housing estates; some social housing, mostly owner-occupied; some for locals, most for incomers. And there is tension. Some do not welcome the new houses and the incomers, the growth of the village. Others see the benefits. But the village changes. In truth, the villages half-died as their guts were torn out when the pits closed and they were left as industrial scrap. But these new incomers are signs and instruments of a new social order, which is coming whether the old village likes it or not. So where might bridges be built? Where do old and new village meet? In the church Summer Fayre of course! Don't laugh, because I can see the elderly women and the young professionals running stalls alongside each other. I can see the children and young people and the 'oldies' mixing together. This is one of the very few places where 'Somewheres' and 'Anywheres' meet, and not just meet but somehow learn to live and work together: kingdom theology in practice.

Given the depressing reality that so many of our churches have no children or young people worshipping among them, we cannot afford to be naive or complacent, but many of our churches still have the capacity to be places of community building. There are many good things about the Messy Church movement, but for me one of the deepest joys is to see older church members, often into their eighties, sitting with children and their families, decorating biscuits. Our churches are places of potential, indeed of existing 'faithful capital'.[19] Despite the scandals that rock the Church – old and new – and despite the fragility of many of our local churches, they, and the Church as institution, still have credibility and the potential to do good. Why does the chair of the (civic) parish council express such regret when the priest leaves the village for a new post? Because the local church is known to do good funerals and professional civic services; to run a Messy Church that feeds some of the local children; to provide a safe and non-cliquey parents and toddlers group; to help to provide open youth work for the young people hanging around the bus stop; to visit at least some of the housebound; to provide a place of prayer and beauty in this village, in this 'place'. This is 'faithful capital' and we underestimate it to our great loss. All of this builds real community and the church with its vicar is at the heart of this work of God's kingdom.

Visible vicars

And what is the role of the vicar in all of this? It is not to do it all. Impossible. I am a terrible cook! No one would let me cook for social events. Rather, it is to help grow and articulate the vision, to affirm others in their doing of this, to encourage them when tired and exercise some pastoral discipline when they are crotchety. And it is to be visible. I had many regrets as I finished my stint as a vicar. One of the sharpest was that I was not visible enough at social events. I think I had picked up clergy resentment at being expected to go to these events. Of course, there are too many to go to, and when life is pressured, playing a Beetle Drive can feel like a frustrating waste of time.

As an introvert, I find them high energy. But I think back to the conversations I had at such events. Mostly uneventful, but real. A few deep beyond words. I think that my conversation partners were more at ease than I was. It was their world I was going into. At the wake after a funeral, or the party after a christening, in the working men's club, I was crossing some sort of invisible Berlin Wall, and I know it was appreciated. It communicated a feeling that 'they' mattered. That 'they' were important and 'good enough' that the Church had sent its public representative to enjoy being with them. And it did matter that it was the vicar who went because the vicar is the visible representative of the Church. It shows that church is part of their community, of their 'place'. Jesus went to loads of parties. Even the solemn Herbert knew that:

> The country parson is a lover of old customs, if they be good and harmless; and the rather, because country people are much addicted to them, so that to favour them therein is to win their hearts, and to oppose them therein is to deject them.[20]

However did vicars get the idea that going to parties was a waste of time?

No one told me during the vocations process that I was going to be a nomad. Anglicans have not taken into their language to the same extent as Methodists the concept of itinerancy. But by the time our son was four, he was in his fifth home. Like most vicars, I have dropped anchor a bit since then but, as I noted earlier, I am something of an 'Anywhere'. I have deep roots, but God has brought me to serve in a part of the country where the minute I open my mouth I am clearly a foreigner – a welcome foreigner mostly. This is not my natural world. There are clergy and other Christians for whom this is their place, and for that I am deeply grateful. I think it is a better model that the leaders of a church grow within it; that they grow within their own culture. But I am more like a missionary than anything else. I have been 'sent' as well as called. And like good missionaries, my task is to incarnate myself within the local culture. So I support Newcastle United – this only alienated two-thirds of my then congregations who supported Sunderland AFC! My capacity to be incarnated in this 'place' was limited mostly by my own inhibitions – as well as living in a four-bedroom vicarage – but I did live there. With my family. This 'place' has been our home where our children have grown up. I cannot be more incarnated than that.

As noted earlier, very few professionals now live on their patch. When I am acting as caretaker or security guard or postman for the church, or when our vicarage has been targeted by local criminals, then I envy colleagues who live in an anonymous vicarage on a housing estate some distance from the church. (I do wonder if the model of vicarages next door to churches is appropriate any more. How can one vicar living in one place but leading three churches live next to only one of them, and should our over-stretched vicars also be caretakers/security guards and postwomen?) But I am sure that vicars need to be visibly present in their communities. They should have at least a public office, perhaps in preference even to a vicarage, where they can be easily seen and found and where they show that they belong. As vicars, we need to pitch our tent visibly in our parishes (John 1.14).

Visibility as a tool of community building is more than a vicarage. Visibility is networking. Do I know the local councillors – do they know the vicar? (I am continually amazed at the people who will give up an evening to come to the institution of the incoming vicar – MPs, mayors, councillors, head teachers. If they come, then what does that tell us about the value they are giving to the C of E and its local visible ministry?) Does the vicar ever go to residents' meetings? As importantly, do known church members go and are they encouraged to do so and not nagged at for not doing more churchy stuff? Do we make our rooms available for community organization meetings? Do I pop into the local shops or pubs with a dog collar on? Am I as vicar in touch with *all* the local schools, not just the church one? Visibility is knowing what is going on. Do I read the local newspaper and follow local events? Do I listen to the local chit-chat about planning applications or where the drugs are being sold? Visibility can be canny. I don't need to be there for the whole event. A flying visit is sometimes better than no visit at all. Visibility must also be electronic. Is the church website attractive and up to date? Can people contact us through 'A Church near you' or is the information out of date? Above all, visibility has feet on the ground. Sometimes, I did get to walk around a bit of my patch with my dog collar on and be ready for a smile or a chat or a bit of banter. Apart from our building, if we have one, the Church has no more public face than ours. Vicars can still help to build community.

Every time we move from a parish we leave a bit of ourselves behind. I have yet to leave a parish and not weep. That is as it should be. I have been allowed to become part of this 'place', of this people. I have been fortunate to serve in communities where there is such a thing as 'place' but, even if I had not, there are people to be loved and gathered, where 'place' can be created. This is part of the Church's – vicars' – responsibilities, as agents of the kingdom.

5

Signs of the kingdom

It's Holy Week. The chair of one of the local community centres phones to ask the vicar to judge the Easter bonnet competition – on Holy Saturday. The chair is wondering why the bishop is too busy to come and do it. The vicar decides not to answer that question. This is a struggling community centre in a struggling village. One of the very few places where community is being built. The chair has been really friendly and the vicar feels a strong sense of loyalty to him and guilt about not doing more in the village, so with a joyful grimace says 'yes'. The vicar decides he is not well qualified to judge Easter bonnets and so takes Mrs Vicar with him. She gives a less than joyful grimace. The judging is done. A couple of people are overjoyed. Others offended. A party starts. The music is loud and the vicar wants to go home, but a family arrives. This family is mixed race in a white village. No Mum at the moment. Just Dad and two young boys and a year-six girl. She doesn't want to be there either; she's really sullen. Never seen her like this before, must be something up. But at least we know each other from Messy Church. Mrs Vicar spends some time making string bracelets with her. She is more content. She feels valued and also like a young adult. A moment in time. A little moment of grace. A little sign of God's kingdom? Not enough, but much better than it might have been. Home to bed ready for Easter Sunday morning.

That little vignette sets up this chapter where we will consider two questions. First, how does the Church discern the signs of God's kingdom in our communities, so that we can join in? Why did I have such a strong sense that supporting that community centre leader was sharing in the growth of the kingdom? Second, what is the role of our churches as 'signs of the kingdom' and within that, what is the role of the vicar as a 'sign'? Why did I drag myself out that Holy Saturday evening to an apparently obscure little social event? And what more was needed to make this more fully of the kingdom?

Discerning the kingdom

As part of our wider theological framework, we have suggested that a key task of a local church and their vicar is to discern the activity of God in a particular community and join in. This is easier said than done. We have already noted that the mind of God and the institution of the Church are not synonymous. Much of the activity of God seems either personal, and therefore hard for us to discern unless we see it up close, or so large-scale that it needs the eyes of a prophet to see it; and some of it is simply hidden from our eyes. The Second Vatican Council made it one of the key tasks of the Church to pray for the Spirit so that we can be enabled to scrutinize the 'signs of the times'[1] and read them wisely. This is not just the *missio Dei*. Indeed, it may be as much a diagnostic vision of a society that is 'going to hell'. But how do we learn to see and hear more clearly?

For a generation now, Anglicans have been committed to the 'Five Marks of Mission' as our guiding principles in filling out the *missio Dei*:

1 To proclaim the Good News of the Kingdom
2 To teach, baptise and nurture new believers

3 To respond to human need by loving service
4 To transform unjust structures of society, to challenge violence of every kind and pursue peace and reconciliation
5 To strive to safeguard the integrity of creation, and sustain and renew the life of the earth.[2]

I wonder if there is a hierarchy here? Certainly, different Anglicans place greater emphasis on different 'marks'. And I have already registered my own perplexity at relating, crudely speaking, a social justice mission and evangelism. I have lived with the tension of individual conversion/social action since my twenties and I am still not 100 per cent sure how to relate them. Is it more important to convert individuals or to engage in social action, if we can express the tension so crudely? The risk of the Church focusing on individual conversion is that we become individualistic and may not tackle wider social injustices. That has certainly been a pattern in church life. What value thousands of converts on an over-heating and doomed planet? But conversely, if the Church focuses on social action, it seems to undermine the importance of the individual and corporate life of faith. What value is prayer and worship in a deeply unjust society with hungry children? So what is the kingdom that local churches and vicars are to serve and make visible? Is it simply *both* service *and* evangelism?

I am going to write down what I *feel* the kingdom looks like, as a former vicar, and then reflect on that.

I feel that the kingdom looks like people becoming more human, children and young people receiving a good and holistic education – in school, youth work and church. It looks like older people, often bereaved, finding new life in community, friendship and purposeful activity. It looks like 'good work', where people find dignity and financial security through their own labour. It looks like functioning families, where there is nurture, and support in the hard times. It also looks like functioning care services, where the health professionals and social care staff can do their job and support and liberate those in specific need. It looks like creation, where people make meaning, in relationships and activities and art. But what happens when I reflect theologically on these impressions?

I have been trained to look for 'signs of the kingdom' through the 'Nazareth Manifesto':[3]

When he came to Nazareth, where he had been brought up, he went to the synagogue on the sabbath day, as was his custom. He stood up to read, and the scroll of the prophet Isaiah was given to him. He unrolled the scroll and found the place where it was written:

'The Spirit of the Lord is upon me,
    because he has anointed me
        to bring good news to the poor.
He has sent me to proclaim release to the captives
    and recovery of sight to the blind,
        to let the oppressed go free,
to proclaim the year of the Lord's favour.'

And he rolled up the scroll, gave it back to the attendant, and sat down. The eyes of all in the synagogue were fixed on him. Then he began to say to them, 'Today this scripture has been fulfilled in your hearing.'
(Luke 4.16–21)

There is good reason for hearing this passage as a wise guide to the kingdom. Luke presents it to us as Jesus' announcement and explanation of the kingdom and of his mission, and the rest of the Gospel shows this being lived out. Every time I read this I am struck by how 'non-churchy' is Jesus' inauguration of the kingdom. Unless we completely spiritualize it (un-biblically), Jesus is talking about actual release of captives and sight for the blind, as well as spiritual release; all the Gospels portray this in action.

I am reminded of the evils that William Temple, the great Anglican prophet of a just social and economic order, longed to see remedied: unemployment or inadequate wages, ignorance, poor quality housing, lack of respect, limitations on liberty and, most poignantly, absence of good leisure.[4]

Even Herbert, from his different age and social setting, reminds us of the bigger 'worldly' vision of God. When he writes about the 'Parson's Charity', he is full of ideas for 'good deeds', which will both be good for the recipients but also be sermons in action. This can feel deeply uncomfortable, but then he writes about making sure that, at the great festivals, all can have a 'good meal suiting to the joy of the occasion', even if he has to sell his own corn to make it happen. And he is committed to be being charitable rather than scrupulous when it comes to helping those who claim to be hungry.[5] Herbert's soft-heartedness subverts his social control. We might not have the wealth to be as bountiful as he was, but the principle of kindness above legalism still resonates, whether we are giving from the vicarage door or from the church food bank. Compassion is still the simplest motivation for displaying kingdom values. And Herbert truly had a wide vision of the work of the vicar, the work of God (for remember he worked 'in God's stead'). So he advised the parson to be priest and also lawyer and physician for his people. This was to include knowledge of the best herbs to use in healing.[6] The breadth of Herbert's concerns is seen most clearly in chapter 32 of *The Country Parson*, 'The Parson's Surveys', when he reflects on the duty of good employment – he regarded 'idleness' as the most pressing sin of his times – but ranges widely over the improvement of the land, being a not corruptible justice of the peace, the best course of action for the younger sons of the gentry, including the European tour. It is a delightful if patrician vision of the wideness of the kingdom of God.

In other words, comparing all this to the 'Nazareth Manifesto', we might say the kingdom looks like 'good news' for those who do not have enough resources ('the poor'), liberation for those who are 'captive' to limited opportunities, understanding for those who have been 'blinded' by ignorance, freedom for those who are 'oppressed' by sadness. If all this sounds 'worldly' it may be because, as we have seen, Anglicans know this is still fundamentally God's world. But is this all that should be said?

I take two further texts as theological norms: '[Jesus said:] "I have come in order that you might have life – life in all its fullness"' (John 10.10, GNB) and 'The glory of God is a human being fully alive' (Irenaeus).[7] I am taking the former in the imperative (commanding tense) of Scripture.[8] If God is essentially the life-giver, in creation and redemption, then this is the clue to discerning the kingdom. But 'life in all its fullness' is a surprisingly opaque phrase. It is a commonplace in current Anglican thinking but we may not have spotted how much we have built on this verse. A brief search of classic commentaries reveals that few of them link this verse to the social liberation of the 'Nazareth Manifesto'. So even Temple interpreted this verse as meaning access to relationship with Christ, who is the door, to Christ as shepherd.[9] The reading is 'spiritual'. As are most commentators. Are we imposing a meaning on this text? A recent commentator provides a more unitary vision:

> Even as Jesus provided wine (2.1–12) and bread (6.1–14) in abundance, so he generously provides abundant pasture, once again illustrating the Gospel's affirmation 'from his fullness we have all received' (1.16) . . . This 'abundant life' is what created life ought to be (1.3–4), and it anticipates the blessings of eternal life. *Abundant life is found at the intersection of created life and eternal life: each is given by God through the Son (or Word) and experienced as knowledge of and union with God.*[10]

The insight that 'abundant life' – kingdom life – is where creation and redemption intersect is profound. It makes sense of the feeling that there is 'more' than social action. And again, the Irenaeus quotation, which has become so popular, can be misused if we do not catch the meaning of 'fully alive'. To be 'fully alive' is to be in conscious relationship with God, Creator, Redeemer and Sanctifier.

Conversion?

A residential unit for teenage mums was opening in the parish. It was not popular and there were planning objections. People were nervous that the young women would attract young men, and that there would be disorder. The parish clergy made it quietly known that we thought this was a good scheme, and visited it early on and were invited to the ceremonial opening.

On this occasion, we were not asked to do anything public, but the very presence of visible representatives of the Church at the opening of this sort of unit seemed deeply symbolic. In previous generations the Church would have been hiding such young women away, possibly even punishing them. Now we were there to bless. Later, I always enjoyed popping in with an invitation to our parents and toddlers group or church events. There was a little frisson when 'the vicar' rang the doorbell. But I will never forget the shy 17-year-old coming to ask for her baby to be christened, or the tear-filled delight in that service. That feels like the kingdom breaking in. But only 'breaking in'.

What of spiritual rebirth? The best bits of parish ministry were when the 'becoming more human' included conscious relationship with Christ. There was an added, energized and big-horizon dimension when that happened. There is literally a light in people's eyes when they know they are loved by Christ. This is more difficult to tell as a story but I find myself thinking of a widow. It was the first deathbed to which I was ever called. 'Jim' was dying from lung cancer. Oxygen was in the bedroom at home. I got there in the afternoon. I imagined I would be on my own, but his family stood at the end of the bed. Conversation. John 14. Prayer. He died that night. I was so grateful that the family kept on at me to come quickly. (Memo to self: the needs of the dying always go to the top of the 'to do' list.) I was also grateful for good training that helped me to cope. The funeral was big and sad but also strangely joyful. And the widow and her daughters came to church the following Sunday (a north-east custom). But they kept coming. And were confirmed. And became active church members. And shone.

Is this better than where Christ is *not* known so explicitly? Is it better even than the young mum coming for the christening?

How can they be compared? But in the life change that comes when an encounter with Christ becomes a relationship with Christ, the answer is 'yes'. This is 'life in all its fullness', life that is a hundredfold blessing to others. This is the kingdom.

I am now convinced that the sort of individual 'conversion' that produces lifelong fruit is the *clearest*, if not an exclusive, sign of the kingdom. I am struck that Temple wrote this, the very last paragraph in his world-changing book *Christianity and Social Order*:

> Above all I would insist as I close that these political proposals must not be substituted for the truths of the Gospel as the mark of the *real Christian*. If we have to choose between making men Christian and making the social order more Christian, we must choose the former.[11]

Temple went on to write immediately, 'but there is no such antithesis'. However, that he wrote this and then went on to assert the distinctive role of the mind of Christ in the Church for assessing social and economic developments shows the weight he gave to the role of the visible Church in a unique role of discernment. The Church is not irrelevant to the kingdom.

The collaborative kingdom made visible

So if all this is anything close to the kingdom, how then does that help us to understand and shape the role of the local church and its vicar?

Remembering that the kingdom and the Church are not synonymous means that the Church does not need to do all of the work on its own. Much of this kingdom work is not now the primary responsibility of the local church; though through our church schools, church youth workers, church social groups, increasingly this is once again the direct responsibility of the Church.[12] But often we can look on thankfully, support personally and politically, and bless.

So the Church can work with, bless, the institutions of the State and civil society that are enabling human flourishing. We can and should work with people of goodwill. I cite them often, but the head teachers of our schools are always instruments of the kingdom who are only too glad of a bit of friendly support from a local church. Some of this kingdom work will be done by individual Christians for whom this is their calling and their passion. Active church members volunteer for community groups in disproportionate numbers. I think of the Christians whom I kept meeting in the Scouting and Guiding movements, or helping at the food banks or credit unions. Some of this kingdom work will be done directly by church-founded and church-led institutions, especially those that properly have a clearer role in encouraging Christian discipleship. And we can never say too often that compassion and the duty of justice are always motivations for kingdom work.

But above all, the Church, where it is welcoming and real, as it cares, worship, learns and prays, is the *best* sign of the new heaven and the new earth. In the quality of its relationships and in that life-giving relationship with God, it is truly a foretaste of the kingdom to come.

The Church's clergy help make visible the work of the kingdom. They are signs and instruments of the kingdom. They are like the dye in the bloodstream, inserted to make things – good and bad – visible. It mattered that the Church's official representative attended the opening of the teenage mum's home. It mattered that the vicar – even if not every Easter! – had attended the party in the community centre. This is the visible and institutional work of the Church that the visible and institutional members of the Church should do. Ironically, and counter to my deepest instincts, sometimes vicars are more important when they show up than when they do something. They cannot and should not 'do' everything but, as we will explore later in this book, they do make visible the presence and blessing of Christ.

An excursus on being visible

I understand and respect why clergy colleagues do not wear their 'uniform'. In contexts where the uniform is an obstacle, because of its associations, then it can be set aside. In our context, where the complexity of relationship between clergy and laity is still unresolved, non-uniformed clergy speak of equality in the body of Christ. But I wonder at the widespread abandonment of our uniform. Are clergy more like the CID or the uniformed police service? Sometimes it is good for us to be 'under cover'. But more often I think we need to take the risk of being visible. Wearing a dog collar in public marks us publicly as 'God's person'. It adds weight to our responsibility but it is also a silent though very visible witness that God has not gone away.

We understand why the police service is organized so that most police officers come by car now. We can still see the police houses that are now private homes in many of our communities. But we also understand why the presence of uniformed police officers walking the streets can be such a reassurance and builds relationships. They may not catch many criminals – so the police service needs to have its ultra-modern intelligence-led operations – but they are signs of the commitment of the State and of our communities to justice and good order. It may be wise nostalgia when people pine for the 'bobby on the beat'.

So what are people pining for when they want to see the vicar as a visible part of their communities: reminders of transcendence, the hope of ultimate good order, the presence of divine compassion? If we ask that question, it may provoke us to answer it in ways other than the hopelessness of stretching the stipendiary clergy ever thinner.

Signs of the kingdom

The new war memorial was being blessed. It was a big civic service. The local MP sidled up to the local vicar at the bunfight. 'You know we are having problems on the N Estate because of the closure of the community centres and youth club. Can you be involved as I do some consultation work, help with some community support and be part of creating a new initiative for the next phase?' I bit back the response that would have said, 'And why are you asking the crumbly old C of E?' and of course said 'yes'. This is kingdom work. This is about rebuilding community, good neighbourhood. But there is more.

We'll call him Alfred. His wife died. They loved one another deeply and had been through a great deal together. He was bereft. He would sit on the bench next to his wife's grave every day. A colleague had conducted the funeral well, with sensitivity and faith. She was able to visit Alfred at home. He already knew some people in the local church. They too had been crucial in making the funeral beautiful and meaningful. He started to pop in to social events at church, and then to church services. Always sitting at the back. Never coming up to receive communion. The vicar visited and struck up a conversation: had Alfred been confirmed? And the story came out. As a choirboy he had once been accused of theft by the vicar and thrown out of the church. Alfred was innocent, and even when the real culprit confessed he could not bring himself to go back to church. He had been betrayed. More hurt from the Church followed during his life, but the compassion of the congregation and vicar softened the hurt. And one day in front of a church full of young people, also being confirmed, he told his story of false accusation and then of coming home. There was a stillness after he finished, apart from the odd sniffle. The story does not have a twee happy ending. Alfred went on to suffer a stroke and several months of sad ill health before he too died. But his funeral service was also filled with faith and that joyful confidence in reuniting life with God beyond the grave. It was a witness to the village of the bloodhound-like quality of the love of Christ. This is clearly the kingdom.

Part 2

WHAT DO VICARS ACTUALLY DO?

6

In persona Christi – and not

I arrived in school to conduct the school Eucharist. (For those not familiar with this, it is a Eucharist conducted in school in a mode appropriate for those present. We discovered that the staff and children who had been admitted to communion appreciated this, and we also gathered a congregation around this celebration.) On the way in, the head teacher introduced me to one of the infant-aged children. A delightful child. Afterwards the head teacher explained that she brokered this conversation because this little girl, when she had heard that it was the school Eucharist, had said: 'Oh, is Jesus (that is, me as vicar) coming again today?' We laughed in a slightly embarrassed way. Of course I am not Jesus coming into school. That uncomfortable ambivalence will haunt and educate this chapter.

In persona Christi?

It is an awesome thing to be the visible representative of Jesus Christ, to stand in as the 'person of Christ'.[1] This is an ancient way of understanding the nature of priesthood and indeed of vicaring.[2] For some traditions in the C of E, it remains a lived reality, especially focused in the Eucharist where this language perhaps makes the most sense. For others, it has fallen out of mind, or been put out of mind. Is it simply archaic and dangerous? As I noted in Chapter 3, it is also my lived experience of catching glimpses of feeling, and much more importantly functioning, *in persona Christi.*

In this chapter we will revisit briefly the traditional language of *in persona Christi* and try to interpret it for our context as part of a wider exploration of the role of sacramental, particularly Eucharistic, ministry in the life of the vicar. But we need to do a little history first within the discipline of Anglican theological method.

We have already noted that Anglicans recognize that the formation of the threefold order, including the priesthood, was a process of historical development that we would argue is a justifiable trajectory from the New Testament – Hooker asserted that the creation of the episcopate was the clearest action of the Holy Spirit in the post-New Testament Church[3] – and is now a settled part of the historic wisdom (tradition) of the Church and therefore a given. But the relationships between the priesthood of the priest and the priesthood of the whole people of God has benefited from more recent reflection.

All ministry is that of the risen Christ, which the Church shares in by the power of the Spirit. 'All Christian ministry derives from and shares in Christ's ministry. There can be no Christian ministry apart from Christ, for his self-offering and self-emptying alone reconciles the world to the Father and people to each other.'[4] This is described, especially in Hebrews, as a priestly ministry. This ministry is entrusted primarily to the whole Body of Christ, who are described in 1 Peter as 'a chosen race, a royal priesthood, a holy nation, God's own people' (2.9). This priestly ministry is primarily praise, though we can amplify it with reference to the worship and service of the churches in the book of the Revelation (1.5–6; 5.9–10) and to Paul's ministry of evangelism and church growth in Romans (15.16). It is not an extensive set of references and, as we noted earlier, is only one strand within a very varied portrayal of the meaning and ministry of the Church in the New Testament. But particularly because of its grounding in Christ's ministry as high priest, this has become very significant in the life of the developing Church.

The language of priesthood in the C of E has not been uncontroversial (Hooker preferred 'presbyter' but recognized its complex associations by the 1590s[5]). But as late as 1986 the C of E could look back to a period when it was widely accepted: 'Christ was uniquely the priest of the New Covenant, but both the Church and the ordained ministry continued to be spoken of as priestly by Anglicans of all traditions.'[6] Until *The Alternative Service Book (1980)*, it was the only liturgical word available to English Anglicans. The C of E had of course substantially revised its meaning in the sixteenth century, away from what it then regarded as a sacerdotal sacrificial priesthood,[7] but the priest remained the one who led the local church, presided at Holy Communion and at the other key rites of passage and was still set apart. Further, as we have had cause to notice, the local priest-vicar continued some of the functions of the traditional priesthood in absolving and blessing. And all set overwhelmingly in a framework of pastoral care. We might say that English Anglicans defined priest as pastor, without using the word.

There is a seemingly obscure theological question lurking behind this discussion. Is this ministry of the individual priest derived from the ministry of Christ in the whole people of God or is it an additional gift from Christ to the priests directly? What is at stake is the long-standing dispute about importance. Are clergy more important than lay people? *The Priesthood of the Ordained Ministry* report made the wider C of E anxious by its use of the word 'special' to describe the ministry of the ordained (though it is Hooker's word[8]) and by seeming to stress the authority of the ordained as coming directly from Christ rather than representing the priestly ministry of the whole people of God. The report argues: 'The special ministry is ordained to speak and act in the name of the whole community. It is also ordained to speak and act in the name of Christ in relation to the community.'[9] *Eucharistic Presidency*, in the different world of the 1990s, expressed this in a more nuanced way:

> We would suggest that, in relation to the people of God as a whole, *the ordained ministry is best conceived as a gift of God to his Church to promote, release and clarify all other ministries in such a way that they can exemplify and sustain the four 'marks' of the Church – its oneness, holiness, catholicity and apostolicity.*[10]

Theologically, I am more comfortable with this understanding but I am forced to recognize that, anthropologically, life can be different.

When might clergy be *in persona Christi*?

Classic Anglican disciplines and modern English Anglican liturgy provide an initial guide to answering this question: the president at the Eucharist welcomes, prays the collecting prayer, absolves, oversees the reading and teaching of the word, gathers the community in peace, leads the great prayer of thanksgiving and consecration, and blesses. These practices have, in part, their roots in Classic Anglicanism; not so much in the liturgical detail – it was simply assumed that the priests would run the services – but rather in the deep decision to stay within the Western Catholic tradition.

We do not now read Cranmer's exhortations to receive Holy Communion worthily. But, having read this in a 're-enactment' of the 1552 liturgy, I was struck by the passion and authority of the plea to receive, made by the priest on Christ's behalf:

> When God calleth you, are ye not ashamed to say ye will not come? When ye should return to God, will ye excuse yourselves and say ye are not ready? . . . I, for my part, shall be ready; and according to mine Office, I bid you in the Name of God, I call you in Christ's behalf, I exhort you, as ye love your own salvation, that ye will be partakers of this holy Communion.[11]

And while the 1662 rubrics for the manual actions during the Prayer of Consecration were inserted then as a method of disciplining the Puritan clergy, they were also simply the majority existing practice.[12] Leading Holy Communion according to the Book of Common Prayer, still the liturgical litmus test for Anglicans, feels like a re-enactment of the Last Supper. We hold the elements and even tear them in imitation of Christ as we say his words.

We noted in Chapter 3 both the theological and the existential basis for the reality of the priest at the Eucharist being *in persona Christi*. I will return later in this chapter to when crucially it is also *not* the case, but for the moment I want to dig more deeply into this.

We have already established that there is a particular linkage between the office of the priest and presiding at the Eucharist. We have noted the impact of this on the individual priest and how this is accentuated when it is the priest-vicar who is leading her people in their celebration of the Eucharist, especially on the great festival days of the Church. We should note how, conversely, this is a source of deep pain when there is conflict between priest-vicar and her people. I remember the gut-hurting pain of administering communion to those with whom I was in conflict. It was the deepest jarring experience in parochial ministry. I think it was because a rupture in relationship, in the body of Christ, at this moment when we were sharing the body, felt almost blasphemous. So what is the reality of being *in persona Christi* at the Eucharist?

Another personal anecdote: as an Open Evangelical I had no anticipation of how much presiding at the Eucharist would mean to me, both very early in my priestly ministry but even now a quarter of a century later. It is truly a privilege too deep for words. So I have come to look to my Anglo-Catholic and Roman Catholic colleagues for wisdom here. I am with Hooker in not wanting to define how Christ is present in the Eucharist,[13] and I struggle with the pomp and circumstance of some celebrations of the Eucharist, which contrasts unhelpfully for me with my imagination of the Last Supper, especially where there is too much ritual focus on the priest, but I am humbled by the sense of reverence for the presence of Christ in more Catholic celebrations. At its best, I am further humbled by how this flows into the lives of these priests as self-sacrificial, holy, joyful living. And where this spiritual dynamic is really at work, it flows into a respect and affection for the priest from the people that inspires tougher Christian discipleship. As an Evangelical Anglican, it is studying the Anglo- and Roman Catholic 'slum priests' that has done more to inspire me in my ministry than any other exemplars.[14]

We also have an inspiring example deep in our Classic Anglican tradition.

> The Country Parson being to administer the Sacraments, is at a stand with himself how or what behaviour to assume for so holy things. Especially at Communion times he is in a great confusion, as being not only to receive God, but to break and administer him.[15]

So the priest is not *in persona Christi* because, in Herbert's words, he is an 'unworthy guest' who must therefore even at a feast receive kneeling. But the priest is also *in persona Christi* as he invites his fellow sinners to Christ's table. And the priest is almost more than *in persona Christi* because he is to 'break' Christ as the bread is torn (and it would have been a loaf of fine bread, of course). Herbert is so conscious of his own sin and unworthiness that his emphasis is much more on Christ as the host:

> You must sit down, says Love, and taste
>   my meat.
> So I did sit and eat.[16]

But Herbert found the strength to stand as Christ at the Eucharist as Christ stood in him. In his poem 'Aaron' he contrasts himself with the holiness of the Aaron model of priesthood:

> Holiness on the head,
>   Light and perfections on the breast,
> Harmonious bells below, raising the dead
>   To lead them unto life and rest:
>   Thus are true Aarons drest.

Profaneness in my head,
Defects and darkness in my breast,
A noise of passions ringing me for dead
Unto a place where is no rest:
Poor priest, thus am I drest.

Only another head
I have, another heart and breast,
Another music, making live, not dead,
Without whom I could have no rest:
In him I am well drest.

Christ is my only head,
My alone-only heart and breast,
My only music, striking me ev'n dead,
That to the old man I may rest,
And be in him new-drest.

So, holy in my head,
Perfect and light in my dear breast,
My doctrine tun'd by Christ (who is not dead,
But lives in me while I do rest),
Come people; Aaron's drest.[17]

So Herbert is filled with Christ, who lives in him, so that he can be as Aaron the Christ-priest, and so invite his people to come to Christ's table. There is a proper ambiguity and ambivalence here, to which we will return at the end of this chapter, but at this point it is worth pausing, as priest-vicars, to allow the depth and totality of this call to speak again. It is for good reason that one of the ritual actions during some Catholic celebrations of the Eucharist is for the priest to beat his breast as he recognizes his unworthiness to be standing *in persona Christi*. But it is also the spiritual rock on which we stand.

I was covering my training incumbent's sabbatical. I remember saying to him: 'Once I get past six Eucharists in a week, I am getting the retireds in. If I do "chips with everything", it will go stale on me.' (Forgive me, my Catholic sisters and brothers!) What I had not yet understood was the granite-like quality of the presence of Christ in the Eucharist. When I was exhausted or troubled or distracted, when words were no longer connecting, then Christ still met and fed me in broken bread and wine outpoured. Sacraments really 'work'. That is why the Church has kept them for millennia. Anglicans believe they are guarantees of Christ's presence.[18] That is why they are so precious.

To put all this another way, the priest-vicar is frequently in a place of spiritual authority in the liturgy: welcoming and gathering on behalf of Christ; pronouncing Christ's forgiveness; overseeing the teaching of Christ; re-enacting the offering of Christ; offering Christ's blessing. Why? What is the impact of this?

These are holy activities, sacramental, where Christ is present in the words and actions of human beings. They are at the same time potentially deep human activities: of relationship and community formation; of honesty and vulnerability; of openness to guidance and to the authority of the other. All done in public and also sometimes in private. Therefore, they are dangerous activities. Dangerous for those who open themselves to these experiences. Dangerous also for those who enact them. Thus they are managed by accountability and, at best, by authenticity.[19]

Again, there is a proper theological discussion behind these actions. Is the priest personally declaring the forgiveness of Christ when she absolves, or is this on behalf of Christ in the

Church, or is it 'optative' – a hope for Christ to act in this way?[20] But the anthropological discussion feels different. Few would slip into a literalism whereby the 'I absolve you' is taken as being the *ipsissima verba* of Christ, and yet these words and actions carry great weight, as I know in my own experience as one who is absolved and also in my ministry of reconciliation; and much more importantly, this is attested to by the Church's practice down the centuries.

So I suggest that it is not an accident of history that our vicars are priests and that priesthood is the best theological category in which to locate vicaring. The priest-vicar makes visible and operative some of the ministry of Christ in the Church and in the world.

'I am not Jesus'

I had had a period of ill health and had to take a break from public ministry for several months. Returning to work was delicate and was carefully managed by my colleagues. But I can still remember sitting in the college chapel, praying before I led the college Eucharist for the first time, and hearing myself say to myself, 'I am not Jesus!' Thankfully I was on my own or else my colleagues might have been more anxious! But I have heard other priests tell me that they have had to say this to themselves, noticeably after a period of ill health. 'I am not Jesus!' This is the dangerous spiritual and emotional counterpart to 'Father knows best' (FKB): to imagine myself to be indispensable or even that 'I am as Jesus to my people'. In the cold light of day, as I write this, it sounds ridiculous, but the power of our calling and the depth of the responsibility can cause us to lose our sense of perspective. I want to reflect on this ministerially and then liturgically.

'No one from church came to see me' was the angry complaint. Someone who had had a serious illness and had returned to church was hurting over coffee. People looked crestfallen. 'But I came to see you.' 'And I came to see you.' 'Yes, but the vicar only came once.' I imagine almost all parochial clergy will have been party to this sort of conversation. We can note here again the historic and current importance of the work of the vicar in person, this representative quality, so that the visit from the vicar is felt as having a weight and importance that visits by lay friends does not carry in the same way. As vicars, we are rightly and anxiously impatient with such comments. It is simply no longer possible for vicars to do all the visiting they would like. Well-organized pastoral care teams are the better response and in time bear fruit in a healthier church life. Vicars are not the only presence of Christ. But there are times when we have to go – at the end.

An older church member was dying in hospital. She had no local family. She was on 'nil by mouth', the now discredited 'Liverpool pathway'. I sat and wiped her lips with the damp swab, which was all I was allowed to do. I stayed too long in terms of a rational use of my diary. But she was dying and deserved having the representative of Christ with her. We must not forget these old disciplines of priesthood in the face of the new pressures.

And liturgically:

> Draw near with faith.
> Receive the body of our Lord Jesus
> which he gave for you,
> and his blood which he shed for you.
> Eat and drink

in remembrance that he died for you,
and feed on him in your hearts
by faith with thanksgiving.[21]

Here we both invite ourselves and others to Christ's table, but as we stand and hold out the bread and the wine in invitation, it is Christ who is inviting the people to the table. Proper ambivalence again. I have built this ambivalence into my manual actions during the Prayer of Thanksgiving. Others of a more disciplined Catholic theology may find this too flexible, but it works for me spiritually and I wonder if this is a journey all priests need to make for themselves. So I always replace the paten and the chalice on the eucharistic table as I say the words, 'Do this in remembrance of me'. I am not being remembered! I step back from the altar a little because it is Christ whom we are remembering, even though he is humble enough gladly to be present through us.

Humility is an elusive virtue: we can never know that we have it. *In persona Christi* is strong meat. As Anglicans, we know that the minister is 'unworthy' but that Christ can still be present.[22] The perils of clerical egotism and pride are ever with us. Perhaps the very moment when I begin even to think that I am *in persona Christi* I am falling. Perhaps this is only safe when it is unselfconscious, when it is shot through with proper theological and spiritual ambiguity. And with a sense of eternity.

Strikingly and perhaps surprisingly, *The Priesthood of the Ordained Ministry*, towards the end of the report, relativizes at the most profound level the role of the priest:

The final chapters of the Revelation to John present a picture of the fulfilment of all things in which the whole company of the redeemed serve God face to face. Part of this picture is that there will be no more temple: God will be immediately present to his people. In other words, there will be no more need for sacraments or priests to mediate God's presence. Thus, whereas those who are redeemed by Christ will be kings and priests for ever, the priesthood of the ordained ministry belongs to the realm which is passing away.[23]

I will in the end be simply Alan again. In Christ.

7

No more FKB
('Father knows best')

I once conducted a straw poll among a chapter of how many of us had been asked to adjudicate on when it was proper to start preparing the church for Easter Sunday. There was, of course, some dissension among the clergy about when was proper: immediately after the Good Friday service? Holy Saturday Morning? Holy Saturday afternoon? But we had all had to take the decision. We laughed. Ruefully. Why should highly trained and relatively expensive professionals be asked (sometimes every year, for some parochial memories are short, when the answer is not popular) to decide on relatively trivial matters, not least at quite a busy time of year? And yet inattention to such matters, as I know to my cost, can result in gorgeous fragile flower arrangements having to be removed from the font on Easter Sunday morning so as to permit baptism and the renewal of baptismal vows.

It is easy in these circumstances to retreat to the old authoritarian ways of 'Father knows best' (FKB), when the vicar (and this applies to all traditions) simply decided everything. But it will not do. This is partly for pragmatic reasons. It is possible to FKB one church or two, but not three or more. But more deeply it is because the Church has rediscovered itself as it has 'rediscovered the *laos*/laity' as comprising the whole body of Christ, of which the ordained are representative ministers. So as vicars we are seeking to build whole self-sustaining and therefore spiritually mature and emotionally intelligent 'communities of the disciples of Christ'. We have undergone a Copernican revolution. The local church no longer comprises the 'vicar's little helpers'. We are body together. In the modern Anglican lexicon, if the first word is mission, the second word is 'collaborative'.

In this chapter we will look at Anglican alternatives to FKB and explore collaborative models of parochial leadership.

Working ourselves out of a job

But I confess to a tension at the beginning of this chapter. During our time in Bermondsey, when we were committed to encouraging 'indigenous leadership', we thought of ourselves as 'working ourselves out of a job'. This was motivated by a comparison with the missionary church overseas, which had set itself the target, however much the reality was different, of growing self-sustaining, self-propagating and self-governing churches. This was the extraordinary vision of Henry Venn, the great Anglican missionary strategist of the mid-nineteenth century.[1] And it was picked up and amplified in the remarkable work of Roland Allen, another Anglican missionary strategist. He argued that St Paul provided a model of church-planting that comprised both travelling apostles and also local teams of elders/presbyters whom he fairly quickly recruited and trained, leaving them in charge when he moved on to the next piece of apostolic mission, even if their leadership skills were still in development.[2]

For us in Bermondsey in the 1980s, we were very conscious that the ordained Anglicans were almost all from a different social background from the host community; the urgency of recruiting, training and authorizing local (indigenous) ordained clergy was great. It seemed an obvious test of whether the C of E was succeeding in inculturating in white working-class communities if those communities were generating their own leaders – as in fact they then did, to great effect. The pioneer in this project was our local vicar, Ted Roberts, who with the support of Bishop Trevor Huddleston had driven this initiative through in Bethnal Green in the 1960s. His justification was simple and still rings true: 'Can a docker be a clergyman in the Church of England? Even if it were possible, is it desirable or necessary? Would it help to overcome the alienation of the working class from the church?'[3]

There is a painful irony here. This then non-standard form of training was disciplined by a geographically limited licence because the wider Church was anxious about 'standards', but it is this geographically limited licence that has now come to be regarded as nonsensical, so the deep point of Ordained Local Ministry has been lost as the training programmes have been suspended. In that respect, it remains the case that the C of E – using the test of growing self-governing churches – is still only partially indigenized in many areas of our country. I wonder if part of the problem is the gulf between what the C of E slowly and painfully learned on the overseas mission field and its settled assumptions about ordained ministry in England. It is of course costly to lead in such a way as to 'work ourselves out of a job'.

However, I can see more clearly now that this was still an essentially Gregorian strategy. We thought we would get the Church right if we got the clergy right.

Collaborative ministry

If we had gone to almost any C of E church until the 1960s, we would have heard only one voice, or perhaps two if there was an assistant priest. Even when there was a memory of the parish clerk leading the responses, it was just the case that the lessons and intercessions, the liturgy and sermon were the work of the ordained. Lay Readers were the exception not the rule and their ministry had been fiercely circumscribed since its revival in the 1860s. This was the old clerical model where the clergy did church and the laity did world. And where there was, as there often was, one ordained man in a parish church, he did it all, Sunday by Sunday. The vicar was 'different'. It was his job to do all the religion so that the laity could be fed. I can still remember the shock of hearing lay people lead the intercessions in a church service for the first time. This is recent history.

We have now recognized the destructive consequences of this model: dependent, immature congregations and exhausted, ineffective vicars attempting to do everything. Our local churches now will mostly only survive if they have a high degree of self-sufficiency, are able to run themselves, to discern their mission, to care for themselves, without intensive professional clerical ministry.

> Until laity and clergy are convinced, based on their baptismal mutuality, that they are equal in worth and status, complementary in gifting and vocation, mutually accountable in discipleship, and equal partners in mission, we will never form Christian communities that can evangelise the nation.[4]

This is more than simply a pragmatic judgement. Remembering that Anglicans do not believe that the New Testament provides us with a definitive blueprint for church order, the C of E has now emphasized both the language of the giftedness of the whole body of Christ, and every member in it, and also that there is a greater diversity of gifts than is captured formally in the threefold order: 'while the number of ordained ministers has declined, there has been a big growth in a variety of lay ministries authorized at the national, diocesan, and parochial levels.'[5] A key skill of the vicar is now working as a team leader and trainer, enabling collaborative ministry.[6] This is no longer the one-person band: rather, it is an orchestra (or at least a little band). The vicar is conductor but does not play every instrument. This, obviously, requires a different mindset and a reshaped skill set. I had to learn the perils of TINA (There Is No Alternative). It became one of my warning signs that I was losing poise when I found myself thinking – well not thinking, just reacting – 'I have to do that.' The better question was surely, 'How do I make sure that task is done?'

We noted at the beginning of this book that this is one of the two great epochal changes in modern Western Christianity – the 'recovery of the laity'. All vicaring now must be done in the light of this. Each ordination service begins:

God calls his people to follow Christ and forms us into a royal priesthood, a holy nation, to declare the wonderful deeds of him who has called us out of darkness into his wonderful light.

The Church is the Body of Christ, the people of God and the dwelling-place of the Holy Spirit. In baptism the *whole* Church is summoned to witness to God's love and to work for the coming of his kingdom.

To *serve* this royal priesthood, God has given a variety of ministries.[7]

If the C of E teaches its doctrine in its worship, then here we have the clearest possible statement that it is the *whole* Church that is the body of Christ, not just or predominantly the ordained. We will have cause to consider later the continuities between the Book of Common Prayer and *Common Worship*, but now we must note this profound, public and timely development. The ordained are one part of the body and some of them have particular roles in building up the body, but they are always integrated into the life of the body. Or are they?

Clerical isolation

Deep in the DNA of the C of E vicar is a fierce independence. For centuries we have been largely unsupervised. The expectations have been intense but there has been little formal accountability. As the internal discipline of the C of E broke down in the second half of the nineteenth century,[8] so 'every man did what was right in his own eyes'.

Positively, this meant that clergy were expected to be both faithful to their calling in their parish and also entrepreneurial. Studying Victorian church-planting revealed a common pattern. Perhaps a bishop would identify an area of expanding population and would persuade the local incumbent to hand over a section to be made into a new parish. Or, more frequently, an entrepreneurial incumbent would drive forward the creation of district churches and then parishes. The new vicar would then be given this patch, and probably a stipend, but would be expected to gather a congregation, build a church, a vicarage, a church hall and if possible a church school, through his own efforts, begging money from grant-making bodies and rich benefactors. That partly explains why so many of our Victorian buildings are falling down. In reality, they were built on a shoestring.

The downside was a continuation of the culture of clerical isolation. Vicars who do not have ministerial colleagues, who do not belong to supportive chapters, who do not have appropriate spiritual and professional supervision, who do not work closely with their lay members, may end up lonely, anxious and depressed. Research into clergy stress and (lack of) well-being shows repeatedly that isolation is a dangerous factor.[9] This is significantly accentuated in FKB parishes where the priest is set apart.

I have not worked in FKB parishes. (Doubtless former parishioners will say the contrary!) But that did not mean that I was immune to clerical isolation. I was getting ready to conduct a baby's funeral. I can still picture the agonized, impoverished council flat where I sat as I heard the story. A new-born baby had died. I worried that this poor couple had had the rough side of medical care, shunted from maternity unit to maternity unit, perhaps not sharp enough to complain. And the baby had died. I was angry for them. I was hurting a lot and trying to cope on my own. Slowly it dawned on me that I had a wonderful team of wardens, a standing committee, a Reader, whom I trusted deeply, but it had not occurred to me to share this burden with them. Why? A deluded sense of clerical self-sufficiency. I then did share some of the story and especially my own sense of need. They were a huge support, of course, and prayed. It made a big difference. But it was a lesson I had to keep relearning.

I am worried that we are still reinforcing old habits of mind by our actions, whatever our words say. When I was instituted as a vicar, I was given the key to the door of the church and my hand was put on it and I rang the bell to signify my acceptance of the responsibility (and, for a time, ownership) of the right to be vicar there. We have to find other ways of affirming the call and authority of a priest to serve as vicar, without communicating out-of-date ideas about vicarly authority.

But still a shepherd?

As vicars, we are called to model ourselves on the Good Shepherd. After the Gospel reading from John, in the Book of Common Prayer the bishop says to the priests:

> And now again we exhort you, in the Name of our Lord Jesus Christ, that you have in remembrance, into how high a dignity and how weighty an office and charge ye are called: that is to say, to be messengers, watchmen, and stewards of the Lord; to teach and to premonish, to feed and provide for the Lord's family; to seek for Christ's sheep that are dispersed abroad, and for his children who are in the midst of this naughty world, that they may be saved through Christ for ever.[10]

The 'treasure' committed to the priests' charge are 'the sheep of Christ'.

This language of shepherding, while richly amplified, is preserved in the new ordination rites. So the priests are urged 'to set the example of the Good Shepherd always before them as the pattern of their calling'. They are called to be 'shepherds', 'to feed and provide for his family, to search for his children in the wilderness of this world's temptations'. And again directly echoing the Book of Common Prayer, priests are to 'Remember always with thanksgiving that the treasure now to be entrusted to you is Christ's own flock.'[11]

The deepest and most sustained imagery of priesthood in the C of E is 'shepherd'. Given the range of models open to

Cranmer and the seventeenth-century revisers, we must note the weight of this. In our interest in charting where Cranmer marked out his priests over against their medieval sacerdotal predecessors, we may have lost sight of the positive choice that he and his fellow Anglican Reformers made. Certainly in the Book of Common Prayer, and still in *Common Worship*, the ministry of the priest is largely defined in congregational terms. At the beginning of the Ordination of Priests Service, priests are reminded that they are 'ordained to lead God's people in the offering of praise and the proclamation of the gospel', sharing with the bishop in the 'oversight of the Church', which they do particularly by sustaining 'the community of the faithful by the ministry of word and sacrament'.[12] Later in the Declaration this is spelt out in greater detail. The priest is to baptize, to nurture, to teach and preach, to preside, to bless and to absolve. The list of responsibilities takes a detour outside the church as the priest is called to 'resist evil, support the weak and defend the poor', but then feels more churchy again as ministry to the sick and dying is specified before finally the priest is called to build up 'the gifts of all God's people'.[13]

We have already noted the ministry of the ordained 'in the world' in Chapter 5, but for the moment ponder this definition of priesthood. It is the priest as carer, leader, enabler. As *Common Worship* stresses the location of the priest within the local congregation, so it reinforces the sense that it is priest and people *together* that form the local limb of the body of Christ. As I reflect on my own ministry as a parish priest, I am struck again both by how dependent I was on the whole local community of disciples in the exercise of my ministry but also that some of the time I operated almost entirely independently of the body of Christ. Some of this I would justify. It is back to the 'Church as institution'. A teaching or social services professional expects to deal with another trained and accountable professional. Indeed, that demonstrates the credibility and reliability of the Church (mostly). But with hindsight I wonder if I might have tried harder to do more ministry together. As a professional among fellow professionals, say when working in a school or with the local council, it was too easy to forget that I was a member of the body and seek to draw in other members of the body. The members of our churches who listened to children read in schools, served as fellow governors, helped to staff the 'Prayer Spaces' and 'Open the Book' were all integral to this ministry. It is the local body of Christ that is the 'sign and instrument' of grace, not just the vicar.

It was especially easy for me to forget this reality, because of my paternalistic personality. I am the eldest son, 'big brother'. I have a lifetime's experience of looking after people. I know in my head that the combination of my paternalism and the need for some people to be looked after produces a mutual dependency, which is potentially fatal for both of us. Other caring professionals have to address their own need to be needed. Why not vicars? I was struck recently by this comment from a wise spiritual director: 'The temptation to want to "fix" everything can be great, but we're not messiahs, though some of us have a deep desire to rescue others and need to be aware of and not be driven by that complex.'[14] I am deeply grateful for my own wise spiritual directors. No vicar ought to be without one.

But why is there such a culture in our church of vicars not seeking proper professional supervision or support? My wife, when she was working as a counsellor, would not go a month without supervision. I used to be able to pass two years between Ministerial Development Reviews. This reflection comes from the same Anglo-Catholic spiritual director (it is doubly note-worthy that it comes out of that tradition):

> by ignoring their own pastoral care aren't ministers setting a bad example? Formal supervision is a clear requirement in most secular, pastoral professions, and no comparable calling leaves the requirement for self-care to the decision of its own personnel.[15]

We have to challenge some of the unspoken, unhealthy assumptions of vicaring and do things differently.

Changed but not taken away

As a curate I was able to spend most afternoons visiting. Such a ministry is impossible for most vicars now. We have to prioritize ruthlessly and organize our visiting. As a vicar of three churches, within a couple of years I had ceased conducting home communions. We had a team to do that. I would only do it on special occasions. My responsibility was to try to ensure that there were teams to provide home communion and indeed wider pastoral care. For many fellow clergy reading this paragraph, this will sound embarrassingly obvious. But we still have clergy who are trying to do all this themselves, and indeed laity who are living with utterly unrealistic expectations of their vicars. So we have to keep saying this, loudly: the vicar cannot and should not try to do it all.

And yet we are back to the pain we noted in Chapter 1. It was a privilege for me to share communion in someone's home. As I write, I can still picture so many of these encounters and the profound relationships that resulted. Was I really ordained to be a manager rather than a provider of pastoral care?

There are many responses to this question. First, even as a busy vicar there were times when I would conduct many of the same acts of ministry that I had done as a curate – perhaps not as often. But this kept me rooted and in touch with my primary vocation. Maybe this should be a spiritual discipline for all vicars as they continue in years or become more senior. Are we from time to time still doing the basic face-to-face ministry of a priest? What would be our real and regular equivalent of the ceremonial foot-washing on Maundy Thursday?

Second, there is a reality that is not often voiced. While people are precious, repeated actions become less so. I observe GPs growing tired as they face the same problems week after week. Vicars get tired too. Even bored. There, I have said it. One of the reasons for moving posts, moving between modes of ministry, even being 'promoted', is to experience new contexts and new challenges. There is a proper sense in which more senior priests may move into more 'managerial' roles. And then perhaps move out of them again as they approach retirement.

Third, this is just how it is. As a priest I may pine for the days of one church, one parish, one vicar, but those days are mostly gone. The Ordinal does not quite call us to that task. It calls us to be shepherd-priests. Not necessarily one-church-vicars. The call to 'reimagine ministry', to 'work collaboratively' is not the same thing as surrendering either the work of a vicar or a priest. It is just to do it differently in this new era. And it still demands gifts and qualities of spirituality and character that are distinctive. Kenotic leadership, leadership that is humble enough to support others in leadership and even to give leadership away to them, requires a deep Christ-shaped foundation.

8

The Chief Exec?

I am sitting in a meeting with my grey vicar suit on. We have just completed a SWOT analysis (Strengths, Weaknesses, Opportunities, Threats) and are setting some SMART objectives (Simple, Measurable, Assignable, Relevant, Time-based). I have recently undertaken an Insights[1] personality and leadership style test (I am an Earth Green with secondary characteristics of Cool Blue) and have twice completed a Myers-Briggs test (my results were I N/S F/T J).[2] According to the psychological profiling test APEST, I am a Shepherd-Teacher.[3] I also have undertaken leadership training programmes. But I still find myself asking 'WWJD?' ('What would Jesus do?').

It is easy to mock. And in an institution that has too often been run in an amateurish and uncoordinated way, we cannot afford to mock. Several years ago we conducted a review of CMD in our diocese. As part of that, we convened a focus group of senior lay trainers, experts in their field, who were all practising Christians, mostly Anglicans. We presented our CMD programme to them. They were warmly supportive but then said: 'We love our clergy, but the problem is that they can't operationalize their theology. They don't know how to help make things happen.' It was a sobering moment.

That could feel like a caricature, but it isn't. There have been so many examples of poor practice within the C of E that it is clear that managerial incompetence seriously impedes the growth of God's kingdom. The children of this world are too

106

often wiser than the children of the kingdom of God. So, when we are reimagining ministry, do we need to think of vicars as chief executives, or perhaps as branch managers with the diocesan bishop as the chief executive? In brief, who 'leads' the Church? And in what style, given that we no longer believe 'Father knows best'.

In this chapter we will explore both the need for leadership, managerial and administrative competence, and also expose why some of this language sits so badly with our deepest understandings of what it is to be a vicar.

Leadership and competence

As a vicar, I was at the head of an organization with an annual turnover of about £180,000. We were responsible for a trust fund that was approaching £2 million. As chair of governors at our church primary school I shared responsibility for an organization with around 20 staff and 240 children. I was also governor of a community primary school and so had responsibilities there for good governance. I chaired a youth project that employed a youth worker. Our own PCCs employed two members of staff and had five more who were self-employed. At its peak, our staff comprised a stipendiary curate, a self-supporting associate priest, a house-for-duty priest, a retired priest, a professional parish administrator, two Readers, two pastoral auxiliaries, several trained lay worship leaders, four organists, six churchwardens, four DCC/PCC secretaries, three treasurers, two lay chairs, several voluntary children's workers and a lay funeral minister who was also my wife. We were also blessed with ordinands most years. I was ultimately responsible for the well-being and good practice of all these people. Together we were responsible for a Grade I listed medieval building and two Grade II listed buildings. As churches, we ran innumerable committees, sub-committees, working groups, many of which I sat on, several of which I chaired. And we were not in my view a major parish.

This is not to mention safeguarding, health and safety or indeed data protection (GDPR), which arrived just after I had left. Administrative incompetence was not an option, though I had *many* flaws.

This is not untypical of the situations of many incumbents, and as the C of E combines its parishes and as we lose more of the one-vicar/one-church/one-parish smaller first incumbencies, so this is becoming the pattern for most vicars.[4] When clergy are asked about stress and causes of demoralization, administrative overload comes near the top of the list.

> Administration and organisation tasks take up the most time: these respondents spent more than three hours a day (or a quarter of their working week) doing admin. The broader research also found that admin was broadly disliked by the clergy and a task in which they often lacked confidence. Results also show that a longer time spent doing admin is linked to a lower level of fulfilment for the priest and lower reports of growth within congregations.[5]

In a moment we will consider ways of tackling this issue, but we need to recognize its inevitability. Vicaring now means managerial and administrative leadership. We live in an increasingly regulated context and there does not seem to be any likelihood that *government* requirements for accountable governance will lessen, or indeed the requirements of the C of E, even given the hope being held out through the simplification agenda.[6] These particular pressures may be new but the pressures of money, time, administration and leadership are not. Reading the visitation returns of Victorian parish clergy shows how many were made ill by the pressures of their era. It is fantasy to imagine that we can escape in our age.

This is why the C of E is right to ask questions about leadership and competence when assessing prospective ordinands. I still remember the coded language we used in our pre-ordination reports at theological college. 'N is addressing their issues regarding organization' meant they couldn't organize their way out of a wet paper bag! We smile but, in conversation with a former CMD officer, I was told about a number of quiet chats with senior lay people expressing concern and even despair at the managerial and administrative shortcomings of their vicar. This is not funny.

However, even the best-intentioned vicars can find themselves in administrative difficulties, bogged down, frustrated and frustrating, demoralized. Sometimes the administrative collapse is a symptom of problems elsewhere with faith or morale or health. Poor administration is often a symptom of physical, emotional and spiritual distress. Or it might simply be overload that has gone on too long. And I am now of an age when the speed of technological change is beginning to leave me behind. So, rather than do the website myself, we found someone else to do it, who had the right skills and took real pleasure in it. This is not to deny that parishes exist where there is little lay leadership with the right skills for these administrative tasks. And it is very often those same parishes – estate or deep rural – that are most in need of outside support. I recently visited a church where a treasurer travelled ten miles from a suburban parish to support a substantially poorer church. Perhaps we need to revisit APEST and add some more initials – Administrator (1 Corinthians 12.28).[7]

There is an important qualification to make at this point: effective leadership is not the same as being a black-belt administrator. As we noted earlier, effective leadership is ensuring that a task – like the administration – is done well, *not* doing it personally. I watch gifted administrators at work with awe. It is not my charism. This is where encouraging and deploying the gifts of the whole Church is crucial. Sometimes vicars are their own worst enemies by failing to encourage and then genuinely delegate. And if there are no suitable volunteers and if the parish is too poor to pay for administrative help, might the locality or the group, team or deanery club together to pay for administrative support? Joint administrators or joint treasurers seems to be the collaborative way forwards.

The necessity but complexity of 'vicar leadership'

But if administrative competence is one area of tension, even more so is the language of 'leadership'. I have seen a visceral reaction against the word 'leadership' among my fellow vicars. Perhaps it is because the Church has sometimes uncritically adopted some of the language of leadership from other spheres? Perhaps it is because there is a perception that Evangelicals have co-opted the language of leadership as a way of subverting or trumping the traditional language of order and offices, of priesthood? Or perhaps it is because vicars have been so demoralized that they have abdicated responsibility for leadership in their churches?

I find this, in part, hard to understand. The concept and even the language of leadership is found in our Ordinals. The priest/presbyter is to share in the oversight (*episkope*) of the Church with their bishop. This is leadership. The priest is to 'preside' and 'lead' in worship, and we have already touched on the linkage between Eucharistic leadership and community leadership. Not acting as a leader for their church(es) *is* an abdication of responsibility by the vicar. One of our Anglican slogans is 'Episcopally led, synodically governed'. Try a little thought experiment: 'Vicarly led, PCC governed'. How does that make you feel? I am personally uncomfortable with it – I would want to place more weight on a team leadership and also recognize the historical weight of the office of church-warden – but the reality is that the Church does need its vicars to lead well, always collaboratively.

We noted at the beginning of this book the crisis facing many of our parish churches and the need for sensitive in-carnated leadership if our churches are to make the transition from the 1950s to the twenty-first century. If the vicar abdicates from leadership then at best the Church will remain static, at worst it will die, leaving frustrated lay members disillusioned and fractious.

There is a further reflection on the nature of 'vicaring' leadership that requires us to take a wider perspective. Our diocese deployed secular life coaches for a period as an experimental method of CMD. They brought something new to the table. I was having a moan about often being the last person to leave the building, and so having to check that the chairs were stacked, the rubbish binned and the lights out. 'All at the end of a very long day!' The life coach was listening sympathetically. She began to reflect on the work she was doing with other 'third sector' professionals – the community centre manager, the youth worker – and how they would say the same thing.

A little light bulb went on in my head. I suddenly saw myself in a new light, structurally. I was the only full-time professional in the building. Of course our people just assumed I would be the last man out. It was a sociological reality, not idleness (they were of course not idle, anyway).

If you are a vicar reading this, how would you categorize your church, sociologically speaking? What other organizations in your patch compare? I decided that our church communities were a blend of a heritage society, an interest group and the WI. It revolutionized how I saw my leadership as vicar. I was a professional leading and co-ordinating three voluntary sector organizations. We look like an authoritarian medieval institution but in fact we are a twenty-first-century voluntary group, trying to offer a professional service. Leadership in this context is persuasive not assumed.

As good Anglicans, our curate and I agreed that we would read *A Country Parson* as a source of theological reflection on our current ministries. The experiment did not last long. The world of George Herbert was at its deepest level so far removed from ours that the leap of imagination defeated us. It was not that Herbert only had a parish of four hundred, the accusation normally levelled against him. No, it was that he could assume that he had authority: 'A pastor is the deputy of Christ, for the reducing of man to the obedience of God. This definition is evident, and contains the direct steps of pastoral duty and authority.'[8] Further: 'The Country Parson is in God's stead to his parish, and dischargeth God what he can of his promises. Wherefore there is nothing done either well or ill, whereof he is not the rewarder or punisher.'[9] As well as his ecclesiastical authority (which in truth was less absolute than Herbert thought), he also had considerable social authority as a minor aristocrat. In fact, it is remarkable how modest is Herbert's sense of his authority and how prominent his pastoral sensitivity – to use our language - in the book. Nonetheless, Herbert is clear that he has the authority to tell people how to behave, including being strict about how people say their prayers in church:

> He, having often instructed his people how to carry themselves in divine service, exacts of them all possible reverence, by no means enduring either talking or sleeping, or gazing, or leaning, or half-kneeling, or any undutiful behaviour in them, but causing them when they sit, or stand, or kneel, to do all in a straight and steady posture, as attending to what is done in the Church; and every one, man and child, answering aloud both Amen and all other answers which are on the clerk's and people's part to answer, which answers also are to be done not in a huddling or slubbering fashion, gaping, or scratching the head, or spitting even in the midst of their answer.[10]

It makes even our most disorderly christening service seem like a Mothers' Union tea party in comparison. Seriously, it should shatter some illusions about the piety of our ancestors. But the point of this quotation is to stress Herbert's authority. I have had on occasion to call for quiet in a christening, but I am wary of exercising this sort of disciplinary authority because of the reaction it provokes. And some of the most common 'bruises' stories I hear from lay people are of the inappropriate and cold exercise of authority by some among a previous generation of vicars. It will take a generation for the memories of those actions to fade.

One of the deep consequences of the child sexual abuse scandals is the loss of authority by 'the Church'. This reality simply has to be accepted. And it means that the only appropriate mode of leadership by vicars now is a humble one.

More than leaders

I wonder if a deeper cause of the suspicion of the language of leadership is that it is too thin. I notice our clergy who are helping to lead their parishes through 'Partnership for Missional Church'[11] enjoy their role in this programme. They normally function as the 'spiritual guide' rather than the leader. That role is most often taken by a senior lay person. As I observe, this is liberating some of the vicars to exercise the sort of ministry that brings them alive and that, I suspect, they imagined they would exercise when they started. There is plenty of 'doing', but more than this is working with the team spiritually, enabling the 'dwelling in the word' and the work of discernment. It is the work that they feel called and skilled to do. In fact, they still exercise a strong and clear leadership function but it is entirely collaborative and they are in a role they relish.

I wonder if there is a clue here to renewal. Christ is still calling women and men into spiritual leadership in the C of E. Perhaps, then, without slipping back into old bad habits, if the Church is to flourish it needs to let its vicars be vicars.

I was not long in post when, as part of a getting-to-know-you and initial-strategy-formation process, we had a discussion in the PCC about roles and tasks. 'What do you want the vicar to do?' I asked. I suspect it was a new question, which I set up badly, but it was quite a brief conversation and a briefer list: leading worship and preaching, visiting, conducting the occasional offices. 'Well,' I said, smiling, 'I can knock that off on Sunday and Monday and take the rest of the week off!' But when we compare that little list to the range of tasks listed at the beginning of this chapter, we can see the gulf between that slightly inarticulate discussion about what vicars are for and what vicars actually do. And my actual working life, some weeks, bore little resemblance to that brief list or even to the Ordinal or Institution and Induction Service.

No job ever quite matches its job description, but when the working lives of vicars and their role descriptions, let alone their generic role description, are so far apart, then perhaps we have identified a problem. Perhaps we do really need to reimagine the role of the vicar: less time at the computer because there is an administrator; less time on the building because there are lay officers and diocesan officials who do that; membership only of selected committees because the other members of the church can be trusted to run them; not preaching or leading worship all the time because there is a ministry team that shares that; not doing all the visiting but working strategically with the pastoral team – all the time leading by facilitating, but also running the nurture group, because evangelism is her core gifting. That sounds like a recipe for a happy vicar.

9

Joy and throne and hair shirt: the Bible and vicaring

We decided to run a short preaching series (in Ordinary Time so as to be obedient to the rules of the Lectionary!) where we would select a short book of the Bible, preach on it on Sunday and follow it up by an open discussion of the same passage at a midweek Bible study group. This was a request from lay members of the churches but we also had a keen curate. I learned a great deal – not just about books of the Bible on which I had never preached (Ruth, Esther, Daniel), but more deeply I redis-covered how the Bible is a source of spiritual renewal. So as we studied Ruth together, I suddenly noticed that 80 per cent of the group members that night were widows. No wonder they connected with the book. I had not paid sufficient attention to this group within our churches. And as we studied Esther, we discovered a new confidence in recognizing different genres in the Bible. We became comfortable in talking about Esther as a 'folk tale' or even a 'fairy story' without in any way denigrating its seriousness as a piece of writing or its place within our own Scriptures. This was more than a piece of technical learning, because as we gained confidence to read the Bible according to its genre so we were able to deepen our trust in the Bible through not treating it woodenly and thus misusing it. Above all, I could feel and see that paying attention to the Bible, both in preaching but especially in this group study, was spiritually renewing. People were hungry to learn. Their faith grew. Their energy levels were sustained. The church felt more alive.

And I realized with some chagrin that this had caught me by surprise. I was a mostly faithful vicar. We gathered as a team to say Morning Prayer each day and often chewed on the Scriptures together, especially when they were a bit like gristle. We preached biblically most of the time. We ran regular study courses. And we even had all three Bible readings in our sung Eucharists. But I had forgotten, somehow, that paying attention to the Bible is spiritually renewing. How had that happened? Was I unique? I suspect not. Do most English Anglican parish churches host a regular Bible study? (This chapter is written for those in that setting.) The Bible had become a hair shirt I was only too glad to slip off.

There were reasons for that. Sometimes the cultural world of the Bible feels a million miles away from the cultural world of our parishes. So much has to be explained before a text can be preached. And sometimes when I was preaching on the Gospel and I would hear the Old Testament or Epistle reading, I would think, 'We need three sermons this morning because those other passages need some explaining.' I do wonder whether we should still be reading all of the Bible in public worship. And sometimes the discipline of the Lectionary itself was a trial. August in Year B. Preaching on 'bread' in John for several weeks. And above all trying not to use the text as a pretext for what I really felt needed saying. The Bible became indeed an itchy hair shirt.

Porridge is good, but is it exciting?

One of the chapters in Herbert's *The Country Parson* that most haunts my imagination is chapter 7, 'The Parson Preaching'.

It begins: 'The Country Parson preacheth constantly: the pulpit is his joy and his throne.'[1] 'Constantly': in bigger churches and with new preachers being authorized, the vicar may not have to preach every Sunday; though she or he may want to. In less well-resourced churches, and especially where there are multiple congregations, the vicar may indeed be preaching almost every Sunday and indeed several times on a Sunday. In one of my former parishes, with four church buildings and congregations, different types of service, including evening services, I sometimes found myself preaching three different sermons on a Sunday. In any case, a lifetime of parish ministry means a lifetime of sermons preached. And if we are to encourage our vicars to stay longer in parishes in these changed times, then not only is the C of E expecting them to preach a great deal to the same people but it is expecting the same people to listen to the same preacher for a long time. 'Constantly' indeed! How then is preaching to continue to be a 'joy'?

The bedrock of Anglican parochial spirituality is the Daily Office. I am very grateful that my theological college drummed this into me and that my training incumbent took this commitment seriously. I was not long into my second post when Evening Prayer became a casualty of busyness. (I feel less guilty about this now. A wise spiritual director said to me once that Morning Prayer is the prayer of the Church. Evening Prayer is the prayer of the priest and her or his family.) It has been my constant experience that Morning Prayer is essential on a working day. Without it the day feels chaotic and unresourced. Morning Prayer really is porridge. It gave me something to live on for the day to come. And Morning Prayer made me pray as a vicar on the days when I was too tired or too hurting to want to pray. The Daily Office is of course largely based on the Bible, so as vowed ministers of the Church the clergy are committed to hearing a lot of Scripture.

I would still defend the value of the Daily Office, especially inhabiting the emotional range of the psalms – joy, thanksgiving, rage, lament – which echoes the daily life of a vicar. And reading lengthy continuous chunks of Scripture is also a good antidote to fundamentalism. A couple of weeks in Judges generated much discussion about the authority of the Bible among the praying team. But I would now acknowledge that the Daily Office does not keep the Bible fresh. Porridge, yes. Spice, no. So what is to be done?

The place of the Bible in Anglicanism

One of the clichés in discussion of the place of the Bible in Anglicanism is that we do not subscribe to a particular doctrine of the nature of biblical inspiration.[2] This is true, but it does not get us very far.

We should first recognize the dominant place of the Bible theologically and thus liturgically in our Anglican inheritance. Cranmer and his fellow Anglican reformers believed they were reforming the Church according to God's revelation: the word of God.[3] So 'Holy Scripture containeth all things necessary to salvation' (Article 6 of the Thirty-Nine Articles). One of the most beautiful and significant of the collects, which Cranmer himself wrote, is that for the second Sunday in Advent:

> Blessed Lord,
> who has caused all holy Scriptures to be
>   written for our learning:
> Grant that we may in such wise hear
>   them,

119

read, mark, learn and inwardly digest
them,
that by patience and comfort of thy
holy Word,
we may embrace and ever hold fast the
blessed hope of everlasting life,
which thou hast given us
in our Saviour Jesus Christ. Amen.

We have noted earlier what I believe to be Cranmer's conviction that it was in common worship, and especially in the public and collective hearing of the Bible, that people were most
likely to encounter God. And for both Cranmer and Hooker
it was the public reading of Scripture even more than preaching it that was crucial; so, for example, the right to preach was
carefully controlled by the Reformation bishops, whereas the
service and Scriptures were read by all clergy.

Hooker, as we might expect, pens another purple passage
about the merits of preaching:

So worthy a part of divine service we should greatly
wrong, if we did not esteem Preaching as the blessed ordinance of God, sermons as keys to the kingdom of heaven, as
wings to the soul, as spurs to the good affections of man,
unto the sound and healthy as good, as physic unto dis-
eased minds.

But as so often, he uses this positive estimation as the platform
to defend the practice of the C of E. Straight away he counter-
attacks the Puritan critique of the 'bare' reading of Scripture
(that is, reading it without always explaining it in a sermon):

That which offended us is first the great disgrace which they offer unto our custom of bare reading the word of God, and to his gracious Spirit, the principal virtue whereof thereby manifesting itself for the endless good of men's souls, even the virtue which it hath to convert, to edify, to save souls, this they mightily strive to obscure.[4]

For Hooker, simply reading the Bible in public was an 'ordinary' means of grace.[5]

The authority of the Bible is recognized in Anglicanism's key texts, such as the Lambeth Quadrilateral, the first article of which requires agreement in seeing 'The Holy Scriptures of the Old and New Testaments, as "containing all things necessary to salvation", and as being the rule and ultimate standard of faith'. Or, as the Canons state: 'The doctrine of the Church of England is grounded in the Holy Scriptures, and in such teachings of the ancient Fathers and Councils of the Church as are agreeable to the said Scriptures.'[6]

But most pressingly in the Declaration of Assent, where all licensed ministers of the C of E affirm their belief in the 'Faith which is *revealed* in the holy Scriptures'. Revelation: in comparison, the creeds simply 'set forth' the faith and the historical formularies 'bear witness' to it. The Bible has a unique authority. And in his brilliant one-paragraph definition of Anglicanism, Rowan Williams writes:

I have simply taken it as referring to the sort of Reformed Christian thinking that was done by those (in Britain first, then far more widely) who were content to settle with a church order grounded in the historic ministry of bishops, priests and deacons, and the classical early Christian formulations of doctrine about God and Jesus Christ – the Nicene Creed and the Definition of Chalcedon. It is certainly Reformed thinking, and we should not let the deep and pervasive echoes of the Middle Ages mislead us: *it assumes the governing authority of the Bible,* made available in the vernacular, and repudiates the necessity of a central executive authority in the Church's hierarchy. It is committed to a radical criticism of any theology that sanctions the hope that human activity can contribute to the winning of God's favour, and so is suspicious of organised asceticism (as opposed to the free expression of devotion to God which may indeed be profoundly ascetic in its form) and of a theology of the sacraments which appears to bind God too closely to material trans-actions (as opposed to seeing the free activity of God sustaining and transforming certain human actions done in Christ's name).[7]

But even given this panoply of authorities, I sense a pragma-tism in the C of E's use of the Bible. The Bible is the vehicle for hearing the word of God, but in such way as is 'sufficient' not total. It is not designed to answer all our questions and there is an honest recognition that there are texts that are hard to understand or accept. The Bible is used extensively in our services, but done so with discrimination and beauty, with rhythm and a sense of the history of the use of texts. Cranmer recognized that even in the work of Reformation the example of the early Church had an important role to play. And of course Hooker taught the Church that the Bible and its inter-pretation and use is inseparable from the life and history of the Church and the proper use of the human mind, reason.[8] After this there is a long and rich history of Anglican reflection on the nature of the Bible, of the meaning of 'revelation' and of how the Bible may be read well.[9] Anglicans do not, at least in principle, have a simplistic attitude to the Bible.

The place of the Bible in the parish

So if that is the place of the Bible in formal Anglicanism, what then is the place of the Bible in the life of the local church and its vicar?

We can return to that shocking word of Herbert, that the pulpit is the vicar's 'throne'. This was partly a reflection of Herbert's conviction that the vicar is there to induce a proper obedience to God, and is also due a proper deference because of his own role. And so the sermon is, at least in part, a time to instil some respect: 'He often tells them that sermons are dangerous things, that none goes out of the church as he came in, but either better or worse; that none is careless before his Judge, and that the Word of God shall judge us.'[10] Herbert advised that as the vicar preaches, so he should 'with a diligent and busy cast of his eye on his auditors' let them know 'that he observes who marks and not'. This is definitely a 'throne'. This feels very alien to the cultural patterns of authority in our churches, though I too have been known to say that the vicar can see a lot from the pulpit.

It is important to note that for Herbert this is a 'throne' from which the vicar speaks with realism, gentleness and wisdom. So the vicar recognizes that 'country people' are 'thick and heavy' (!), and so leavens his sermons with 'stories and sayings' that they will remember. While the vicar is to use all his learning and skill in preaching, the most important element will be that it is 'heart-deep', full of expressions of faith to God and care for the situations of the parishioners. And of course he does not preach for more than an hour! Because if someone hasn't profited in that time, they will profit less if the sermon goes on even longer.

If the language of a 'throne' feels archaic, it triggers for me three slightly contradictory reflections. The first is that we underestimate the authority of the pulpit to our detriment. I have noticed how many of our best lay preachers prefer to speak from the lectern rather than the pulpit. There is an instinctive sense of the weight of responsibility which is associated with preaching. I watch gifted communicators, teachers often, struggle with a 'sermon' because they do not feel they have the authority to speak. The C of E is wise in its careful spiritual, educational and formational selection and preparation of its preachers.

We were having a run of 'difficult' funerals, suicides. Young men. Eventually, in one of my funeral sermons, I said to the church full of young people: 'We have to stop meeting like this. Look at the pain that suicide causes (with the broken family sitting at the front of church). Talk to someone. Talk to us. But please don't do this.' I hope it didn't sound like a telling-off. It was a plea from the heart. But the funeral director, half-teasing, would say to me in the following months: 'Well you told them, Vicar. And it stopped.' At least for a bit. But he for one never forgot that sermon.

My second reflection is a confession that I have abused the pulpit. I have a tendency to nag. Part of the discipline of parochial preaching is precisely speaking truth to people whom we will meet over coffee, and over coffee next week and so on. It is shining a light on specific issues in local church life with the word of God, and that can be very uncomfortable. This is not the same as the vicar nagging about commitment, or backbiting, or money – from six feet above contradiction. I was guilty of that. Again I was blessed when a new curate arrived and, without saying anything, just preached differently, positively, about what Christ gives, not about how *you* are failing him. The throne of the pulpit is not a place of manipulation.

The third is a slightly nervous reflection: that God still speaks powerfully through the Bible. We were preaching our way through Daniel and it was Belshazzar's feast this Sunday. But it was also the pre-Brexit referendum Sunday. The twin themes of being alert to hubris and so being able to heed 'the writing on the wall' made the hairs on the back of my neck stand up, even as I was preaching. I am frequently surprised – and therefore I should not be surprised – when a sermon speaks to a person or a congregation. 'It is as if God were whispering in my ear.' Here the throne of the pulpit truly is God's throne and we are, mysteriously and humbly, the PA system.

So, to attempt to systematize this, we could say that the Bible is primarily a means of encouragement, where the loving grace of God is communicated. It is formative of the character and mind of Christian congregations, as it is read and pondered week by week; though one of the most depressing aspects of vicaring is to have to see the huge gulf between what is read in church on Sunday and what happens in congregational life during the week. And it is still the place where and when God speaks. God sets our priorities in the reading of Scripture, both foundationally in terms of trust in Christ and in Christlike living – hence we stand to hear the words of Christ in the Gospel – and often by placing a finger on a specific issue in the life of a church community or individual for that day. All this has left me with a more dynamic theology of the Bible. It does not function best as a rule book or systematic theology text-book. It does function best when we let God speak through it. Who would have believed that an obscure verse from Leviticus about jubilee would become the spark to ignite a global move-ment of liberation from debt for millions of people? This is a rather unsystematic systematic theology of the Bible.

I am struck by some of Hooker's most remarkable reflec-tions on the nature of biblical inspiration. In a long section contrasting the nature of law in Moses' ministry and that of Christ, Hooker makes the surprising point:

> Moses had commandment to gather the ordinances of God together distinctly, and orderly to set them down according unto their several kinds, for each public duty and office the laws that belong thereto, as appeareth in the books themselves, written of purpose for that end. Contrariwise the laws of Christ we find rather mentioned by occasion in the writings of the Apostles, than any solemn thing directly written to comprehend them in legal sort.[11]

This is part of a long argument, both negatively denying the permanency of some of the laws in the Bible and positively arguing that God allows, indeed encourages, change ('mut-ability') in the governance of the Church. In passing, Hooker makes this point about the nature of law in Christ's own teach-ing: that it is not detailed or easily translated into regulations, but is dynamic and designed to generate development. Moses wrote, and wrote law. Jesus did not. The more I think about this, the more astonishing it is. Hooker was clear that the Bible had one overriding purpose:

The main drift of the whole New Testament is that which St John setteth down as the purpose of his own history; 'These things are written, that ye might believe that Jesus Christ is the Son of God, and that in believing you might have life through his name' (John 20.31).[12]

The point of the Bible is to take us to Jesus, in a life-giving and dynamic way, and keep us there.

The joy of the Bible

How do we stay fresh – joy-filled – about the Bible? I offer some suggestions based on my experience as a vicar and now as a CMD advisor.

First: the Church needs to make best use of its biblical scholars. There are new treasures to be found in the Scriptures but it can often take a special expertise to find them. This special expertise needs to be nurtured. Cranmer recognized the need for 'doctors' who would explore the 'high mountains' (Cranmer's phrase) of the Bible.[13] I have sat and watched my sister and brother clergy, and Readers and lay ministers – everyone! – be visibly refreshed as they are guided by a biblical scholar, like thirsty people in a desert. So regular Bible study of the highest kind is now part of our diet for CMD. And this can counteract the next cliché, that you can tell when a vicar trained from his or her bookshelves – nothing new since . . . This will not be the case if regular high-level Bible study is part of our diet.[14] (This poses interesting challenges for biblical scholars, whether they have something to say of relevance to the front line of the Church.) Each Christmas I would read or reread a critical study of the nativity narratives to keep me from either slovenliness or cynicism.

But I have no time for counsels of perfection here. In my second curacy, I made an important journey when it dawned on me that there were bigger congregations for the occasional offices than for evensong: where did I need to invest my limited preparation time? This was so contrary to the rhetoric of my own training, which seemed to imagine that a vicar had hours a week to prepare for each sermon – not in a busy parish with many human demands to be met. So there is a pragmatism here of the 'good enough': for a big set-piece sermon, commentaries, time in the study and a printed text, but for the midweek Eucharist, prayer, a few minutes of quiet and handwritten notes is appropriate. I learned to trust that it is God who is faithful. And perhaps the deeper preparation is long-term biblical study rather than a hurried glance at a commentary.

For the big sermons I still follow the teaching of Bishop Ian Cundy, presented on a wonderfully amateurish OHP slide of a house, that we should go in through the front door of the text on Monday morning, so (to change the metaphor) the text had time to stew before we wrote the sermon ('stewed' sermons were always better than a 'flash in the pan' or a 'ready meal' sermon); that we let the light of commentaries and also of the world in through the windows. I think the walls and the roof meant something, but certainly heat and light came out of the chimney!

Second: Bible study with groups of clergy can be deeply frustrating. Different traditions, training and personalities can all contribute to a clash of egos rather than an encounter with God in the text. What subverts this is the use of the methods of *lectio divina*, the modern practice of prayerful reflective Bible reading, used both collectively and individually, drawing on monastic traditions.[15] Again and again I sit with sister and brother clergy, and the disciplines of silence, simplicity, attention, self-awareness and above all prayer enable a listening that bypasses the ego and allows the journey into the *second naïveté* of Bible reading.[16] This can work in chapters too. A brilliant area dean introduced into our chapter meetings the practice of a brief Bible study on the Gospel for the following Sunday. Self-interest provided the initial motivation, followed by wonder as the different insights from colleagues brought a passage alive.

Third: it dawns on me that perhaps I had become a little stale in my use of the Bible because I was not using it. I learned a valuable lesson in my second curacy from my predecessor. It was a former pit village and attendance at funerals was large. So he had kept a note of the text he used for each sermon and developed a library of funeral sermons. I failed to follow his administrative excellence but I tried to learn from his example of variety. Perhaps today's funeral is best enriched by a reading of John 14? But perhaps it isn't? Perhaps the family of the old soldier from the Durham Light Infantry will be blessed by the passage, 'Fight the good fight' (1 Timothy 6.12) because that is the hymn of the DLI? Or a sermon drawing on the love of Jonathan and David for a bereaved gay partner? Or 'the winter is over' from the Songs of Songs (2.11) for a second marriage after a painful first one? This could be game-playing or it could be a genuine attempt to let the Bible speak into a current human situation. Use it, or lose it.

What is missing?[17]

When I reflected on why I had become stale in my use of the Bible, I had to realize that it was because I was not reading it enough with other people, including wise scholars in their commentaries, but also much more widely in the community.

We used 'Godly Play'[18] materials in our school confirmation class. This day, we were reflecting on the story of the Exodus, a good baptismal metaphor I thought. The children, of course, got the point, but in the 'wondering' one of them asked: 'I wonder how the Egyptian mothers and wives felt?' Not a question I had ever been asked before. Not a question classically asked in the canon. But an apt question and one deeply of our time.

Most seriously, I realized that I was not reading the Bible enough with people who were curious about Jesus. I had been rightly taught that every church should have a regularly scheduled enquirers/nurture group. The closest I got to this most years as a vicar was the annual confirmation class. They were always good experiences. Most people in the room were there because they wanted to learn, were feeling a need for a deeper commitment. And apart from the questions, the best parts were often time spent pondering an episode from the life of Jesus.[19] He remains both an attractive but also sometimes a baffling figure and these studies were never wooden or artificial; though there is often much work to be done connecting Jesus of Nazareth with the Christ of the Church. But there was joy in the Bible in these sessions.

Perhaps Herbert's joy is to be found as we honestly wrestle with the Bible together and let it lead us to Jesus.

10

Sacraments of the present moment

The curate was debriefing with the vicar about a recent christening. The curate, perfectly properly, had arrived in the parishes with considered understandings of the meaning of baptism, including infant baptism. These were then tested as he began to conduct 'christenings'. This particular christening was of the child of a single (deserted) mum from one of our poorer streets. Her flat was ill-equipped and shabby. It was not one of the huge social-occasion christenings with many guests and a glitzy party. But the curate reflected afterwards: 'At least she knows now that God loves her baby and her.' The vicar knew that the curate had got there.

Why should we do occasional offices?

As a curate I agonized about the integrity of the promises that people were making in baptism services or about the integrity of saying the words of the Christian funeral service over the body of someone I did not know and who had not evidently been an active member of the Church. Successive parish churches where I ministered tried various tactics to draw the beneficiaries of these occasional offices into active Christian discipleship. I think of a variety of 'baptism policies' – home visits, the use of teaching DVDs, compulsory church attendance – but none had a huge success rate in terms of attracting new church-committed Christian disciples. Though, taken as a whole, *occasional offices remained the most fruitful path through which people grew in faith*. But even if the occasional offices did not mostly lead to active Christian discipleship, this is not a defeatist way of saying it wasn't worth bothering making them as good occasions as they could be in terms of embodying Christian compassion and faith. And nor did most of these occasional offices feel fraudulent. There was almost always an integrity about the relationships and about the events in themselves. How do we make sense of this? I found four tools helpful.

The first was the realization that there is no perfect way to conduct Christian baptism. The New Testament does not provide a neat blueprint for how to do it. The decision to baptize the children of 'Christian' parents may well be found in the story of the Philippian jailer (Acts 16.33), but Hooker recognized that the practice of routine infant baptism was a post-New Testament pattern even though he regarded it as normal and completely defensible.[1] For Anglicans this is significant. Where there is no definitive scriptural mandate, the Church, guided by the Spirit and using its reason, has the authority to decide its practice. Further, the Church has administered baptism in a variety of ways: at the point of a sword, at one end of the spectrum, and after conscious free adult choice at the other end. Both were deemed worthy by those who conducted them! And it is not so long since the C of E regarded mass infant baptism as a crucial tool of mission. In the chaos of the rapidly growing Victorian cities, contrary to our assumptions, many babies were not baptized. Missionary Anglican clergy would seek out these children and persuade the parents to have them baptized (christened). A fiery Evangelical vicar, William Allen, in Bermondsey, is famous for baptizing 100 babies in one day and paying for the curate to visit door to door to find the children. And, of course, these baptisms were often conducted on weekdays, with just 24 hours' notice and with only the parents and godparents gathered around the font.

So it may be worth reflecting on how we conduct baptism now, if our key task is to provide the sort of welcome that facilitates an encounter between Christ and the immediate family, as well as their guests. We should remember that our recommended pattern of trying to conduct them during the main act of worship on Sundays is the Church's *current* strategy in our context. It is not infallible or universal or timeless – or perhaps always wise and kind. How hospitable is it to require non-regular churchgoers to sit through a lengthy liturgy, much of which may not be easily comprehensible, if we insist on baptism in a sung Eucharist? I can still see the baptism parties leaving at the Peace because they naturally assumed that warm greetings and handshakes and hugs marked the end of the service, not half-time. This may be different if our liturgy is not rather inaccessible (which is, of course, another conversation . . .). There are great benefits to both family and congregation when a child is baptized and welcomed, surrounded by the local people of God in a joyful act of worship. But there are also benefits of conducting baptisms with just the family and their guests. We could make each service more personal, with the talk connecting with the stories we had heard about the child. I know clergy who will produce a special PowerPoint with photographs of the child, or a special order of service. We were often baptizing adults because they wanted to be godparents, and this worked beautifully in a family-shaped service. We tried to balance the absence of a congregation by having little teams of lay baptism vergers, or visitors who were known and, especially in villages, would meet the family naturally in other places. I learned to be flexible in an appropriately Anglican way.

Second, it matters that we take seriously what people are bringing to the event. When I was researching into working-class attitudes to the Church in the late nineteenth and twentieth centuries, one of the phrases that leapt out from the interviews was 'you go when you need to'. The C of E in working-class areas of England was normally 'socially superior'. Certainly the vicar was. And in many places it was on the side of the Establishment and the bosses. So it was an institution to be treated with some caution and not too much respect – especially if one believed in the second popular saying: 'You don't have to go to church to be a Christian.' So a family would come to church seeking what they wanted and not immediately malleable to the Church's wishes. My experience suggests much of this is still the case in my context. I think of the surprise of one father when it dawned on him that we anticipated staying in touch after the christening: 'I never thought that having N christened meant having something to do with the Church.' This was not said unkindly.

More positively, people are coming to these occasional offices with quite strong operative theologies. They may be inarticulate according to the standards of degree-educated clergy, but this is often significant 'ordinary' theology.[2] They tell us that christening is about becoming a member of the Church; that in christening God is promising to bless and protect their child.[3] Who am I to despise this?

As a curate, I dreaded baptisms. This was mostly because managing a main Sunday morning service with up to three baptism families (and guests) was a logistical nightmare, but also because the baptism visit itself had an uncomfortable dynamic. I would be warm and coo over the baby, and ask them what they were looking for out of the baptism, but then, in effect, tell them what it was *really* about, often ignoring what they had just said. It took a smart research student curate to teach me to listen respectfully and to try to build bridges to where the family was.[4]

Slowly I put this together with my Anglican ecclesiology. If we truly believe in a 'modest' Church,[5] then we will both witness to what we see and know of Christ and will also listen carefully to how others see things, wondering how the Spirit is active in their lives (if we really believe in the *missio Dei*), and we may not believe that the Church has a monopoly on truth. Unlike so many of our forebears, humility may be the key quality for the clergy to exercise in occasional-office ministry.

I carry the memory of one particular funeral. This was a family I did not know. I was covering for a nearby parish during a vacancy. It was a 'straight-to-the-crem' funeral. The man who had died seemed to spend most of his time watching the horses on TV – with a financial interest. It was very hard to know what to say in the funeral address by way of celebration of his life. With hindsight I should have spotted that his family were still shocked in grief and so could not really answer my questions. When I went back to see them afterwards, much more about his life came out, including the years he had spent as a choirboy and how much that had meant to him. I had had no idea. It would have been easy to treat this life with some disdain: 'He just gambled and watched the telly.' Instead, a vista of experience of God and foundational faith opened before me. I did not know this man. I had been preserved from judging him only by the discipline of Jesus and the Church – 'Do not judge, so that you are not judged yourself.'

All this is framed for me by a piece of old Anglican wisdom, which has fallen out of our collective memory – the 'charitable presumption'. I was first introduced to this by the deeply Anglican Evangelical biblical scholar Dick France.[6] The wisdom is that we take at face value what people say to us. The C of E is not the 'Spanish Inquisition'. It is not the job of the clergy – note the classic English post-Reformation anti-clericalism – to pry into the souls of the laity. And more deeply, we are to give people the benefit of the doubt. This always has to be managed with parochial common sense but there is a presumption that we are to respect people.

This must be linked to a passionate theology of welcome. While the Book of Common Prayer can feel off-putting with its relentless focus on sinfulness, somehow this was transformed into a joyful open-armed theology of welcome in Herbert and in later Anglican theology and spirituality. This is most perfectly exemplified in Herbert's poem 'Love bade me welcome'. As I have written elsewhere: 'Eventually, the enthusiastically and recklessly forgiving God of the parable of the prodigal son has moved to be the controlling image of God in Christ for Anglicans.'[7]

My third tool is that I learned not to be overambitious. In my imagination, during these baptism visits and christening services, people would be so moved by the Spirit (and my own ministry!) that they would come to put their faith in Christ. Slowly it dawned on me that I would not buy anything from a stranger, however nice, at first acquaintance. If I acted like a Spanish timeshare salesman, I would be treated as such. Much smarter was to discern where a person was and meet them there. Reading one of the 'evangelism scales' helped me to realize this.[8] Was this person already familiar with Christian language and thus able to understand talk of baptismal regeneration, or was all this deeply unfamiliar, in which case what might be a *realistic* next step for them? I realized slowly that even the word 'God', which for me carries meaning of personal love as well as mystery, might mean something entirely other to someone else: an impersonal power, perhaps, as in 'May the force be with you.' For someone for whom God had been an impersonal force, to be able to learn and even experience that God is personal would be a huge step.

One unmarried economically disadvantaged couple I went to prepare for a christening asked me at the end of the visit if it would be a 'normal christening'. Slightly anxious, I explored. They explained to me that at the last christening they had attended, they had all been made to kneel at a rail and were given bits of cardboard to eat. It could be tempting to despise such ignorance of the Christian faith, or to ask slightly primly why such people were bringing their child for baptism. The response is obvious. These are the very ones who are most precious to Christ. They are coming with longings and hurts, probably more so than the more articulate couples. And baptism is *the* sign of Christ's love for them and especially for this child. We were able to stay in touch with this couple through many travails. When I left, the child was well established in our church primary school.

I am not convinced that the Anglican Reformers quite knew what to do with infant baptism. It might wash away the effects of original sin but that was not the same as predestined justification and sanctification. As with the burial service, their instinct was to keep the Church inclusive and catholic. So infant baptism was retained. But it was more than just retained. Article 25 asserts that the sacraments are 'effectual signs of grace'. In other words, they deliver what they promise. Article 27 asserts that baptism is both a 'sign' of rebirth and an 'instrument' of being grafted into the Church, to such 'as receive it rightly'. The baptism service in the Book of Common Prayer is focused on the child not the beliefs of the parents. This should still be the focus of kingdom parish ministry, which has a wide perspective alongside the joy and duty of gathering new disciples.

It had looked like a routine but lovely christening. A young family from a poor social housing estate. Three children to baptize including a junior primary girl, 'big sister'. She was excited and engaged during the visit. But on the Sunday they were late. Very late. And then the dad's mum arrived. Cross. Embarrassed. There had been a row and 'she' (the children's mother) wasn't coming. Sure enough, the dad arrived on his own. He was in tears, a tough young County Durham man. And the kids were pale and drawn, including 'big sister', who of course was dressed like a little princess. We did our best to make it as beautiful and normal a service as possible, including a special role and gifts for the big sister. I conducted the service holding back the tears, and cried afterwards. I tried to do a follow-up visit soon but it took several attempts before I found them in. 'Everything's fine, Vicar . . .' I checked in with the head teacher at the girl's primary school and made a fuss of the girl next time I was doing an assembly. I discovered that she had gone back into school talking excitedly about her christening. But my heart still ached for them. I had done the little I could. It is down to the mystery of God's love now.

As well as humility and modesty, a fourth tool is needed if we are to undertake classic pastoral ministry effectively: faith.

Faith that this is indeed God's world and that God is active in it. Whether we label this the *missio Dei* or 'prevenient grace', it does not matter as long as we remember that grace goes before us and that it is in grace that we trust for ourselves.[9] And there is faith that God hears the prayers of the Church, and of the family, and honours the promises made on God's behalf in the service.

Intriguingly, the Anglican Reformers had a clearer sense of the other occasional offices. Marriage was for procreation and was a defence against sin, though it was begrudgingly allowed also to be an opportunity for love and comfort. In making this rite accessible and also a beautiful occasion, using language that has worked for couples down the generations, the Reformers continued the wisdom of the Church that marriage is a 'gift of God in creation', given by God for all and that all can celebrate with God's blessing.[10] This remains fundamentally God's world.

The Reformers also defended the saying of prayers and the reciting of the promise of the Resurrection over almost all the dead, contrary to the 'Puritans' who wanted this comfort only given to the elect.[11] This is in keeping with Cranmer's reserve about predestination. As the Church of and for the English people, over-strict boundaries were and are inappropriate.

'Sacrament of the present moment'

The phrase 'sacrament of the present moment' is not original and has its origins elsewhere.[12] But it seems very apt to describe what is happening in these occasional offices. They are sacramental moments, when in the often chaotic mess of life, God becomes actively and visibly present through welcome, relationship, compassion, action, some words and the formal sacrament. They are touches of grace, often life-shaping, normally important, but not always full of longevity. Especially in a busy parish, there are many more occasional offices than can be followed up. And, as we noted earlier, for some people the service is enough. That is what they wanted the Church for, that moment in time when, often, no one else would do. Rightly, we struggle with this. Compared to the long-term, life-changing relationship with Christ, these fleeting encounters are 'second best'. But they are still good and important. Perhaps we would do them better if we understood them more realistically.[13]

I am not good at names and, anyway, babies often look the same! So one of the tricks of the trade is to learn to enthuse over babies: all babies are by definition beautiful, even if they are not. But the families would remember me. Or they would remember which one of my colleagues had conducted the christening, or wedding or funeral, because for them it was a unique event. Little Johnny or Julie would only be christened once. Dad only had one funeral. That was what made it such a special occasion. (I learned a lot about the importance of these occasions by looking at the invitation cards, especially for christenings, or the funeral notices in the newspaper; and at least one bishop's secretary of my acquaintance read the funeral thank-you announcements to see which clergy were doing a good job!) On the other hand, the clergy involved will have lost count of the number of occasional offices they have conducted: 'This is yet another one . . .'

This takes us to the heart of one of the deepest challenges of vicaring. What for us is a routine event is for the family almost always vitally important. The relationship we build needs to be warm and authentic, but it is a relationship to us in role. I never felt more 'in role' than in an occasional office.

Christian 'shamans'

I was sitting idly making notes in a lecture on anthropology. The professor was talking about shamans. I thought this was a little off the park for the Christian doctoral programme we were running but, suddenly, I was rooted to my seat. The professor was describing the role of the shaman. Living slightly outside the tribe, a bit detached, certainly unusual. This is the person to whom the bereaved go. This liminal person walked with them through the journey of death, funeral and grief, until they could be reincorporated into the tribe. The parallel is not exact – and the word shaman is not an entirely comfortable one because some aspects of 'shamanism' can be very problematic from a Christian perspective – but it dawned on me that from the viewpoint of an anthropologist, I was a Christian 'shaman'. People came to me (us) because I was the odd person who lived outside the normal, but who could therefore walk with them through this abnormal state until they were ready to re-enter normal life. This was my role. So it mattered that I looked the part. It mattered that I was in some ways strange, 'holy'. This odd moment in a lecture liberated me. Instead of trying to make every occasional office into an opportunity to 'preach conversion', I realized that my role was to walk with people through these profound life moments. But to do it Christianly. My role is to be a Christian 'shaman', a Christian minister, a Christian priest, a Christian vicar.

If I kicked against the role, I was just causing deep confusion to others, and probably hurt, and certainly living with constant resentment myself. But if I relaxed into the role, and then tried to live this particular role in a Christlike way, I was both more authentic and more nimble. This role is a human reality. Societies have people who do this stuff. In our society the people who do this stuff are often, just, Christian ministers (thank God). So we can do it well with a clear conscience. Which is good news, because for many stipendiary parish clergy this remains a large part of the working week. If, as we know, the number of occasional offices is dropping, then perhaps this is an opportunity to do them better. Perhaps we might even compete effectively with the competition.

What does it mean to do it 'Christianly', in a Christlike manner? It means patience and generosity, even with the irritating. It means naming Christ. It means surrounding the people and the event with prayer. It means being sensitive when walking with people through this life event and trying to facilitate a journey of faith as well.

Occasional offices are still a key task of the Church – witness in recent years the effort the C of E has put into understanding them and increasing our commitment and competence.[14] Any sense that we are doing people a favour by allowing them access to these rites, or talking down to them, or doing them indifferently, is missional suicide. This is another front line in the war with secularization. Occasional offices, more than any other activity of the Church – apart from the great televisual events – keep the rumour of God alive and provide an alternative narrative to that of the media: 'Well, the Church may be old-fashioned but, the vicar – she was really kind and alive.'

There are three perils for 'stretched' vicars in occasional-office ministry. One is that we become insensitive to the people involved. I knew it was a warning sign that I was getting emotionally and spiritually tired if the funeral visit just felt routine.

The second peril is that we lose energy for having a real conversation about faith. One of the privileges of receiving curates is precisely that they arrive not yet ground down. They come with hope and therefore expectation. They expect to talk about faith and God on occasional-office visits. I am deeply grateful for the gentle challenge they posed to me when my occasional-office practice had become in effect hope-less. I have recently been encouraged by the questions that the organization Leading Your Church into Growth suggests we might explore during some occasional-office ministry: 'Who are you? Where are you (with God)? Who don't you . . .?'[15] We will explore clerical hesitancy to talk about God in Chapter 11, but I sometimes had the feeling that the people I was with were *expecting* me to talk about God and to pray, more than I was. When we offer welcome in the name of Christ, we are also to offer Christ.

The third peril for clergy is that we think we undertake this task alone. I was only available for even 'crem funerals' because the Church (people and institution) had paid to train me and paid me to be available. Christenings, weddings and funerals all required lay teams – dedicated and skilled lay teams – in buildings sustained by Christian communities. And while some of the specifics of this ministry have to be undertaken by the ordained, this is not always the case and does not have to be exclusively the case. The Church is catching up with funeral celebrants by training and deploying its own lay funeral ministers, who as well as being additional resources, are also a fresh kind of resource. Do the clergy always have to do the talk at the baptism service or run the marriage preparation course? I was not a solitary Christian 'shaman'. Or, rather, when I imagined I was, I lived without the support of the rest of the body of Christ and offered a model of discipleship that was badly skewed. Richard Hooker argued fiercely with his Puritan opponents for the right of the Elizabethan midwives to baptize sick babies.[16] The sacrament of the present moment is partly linked to the person in the dog collar but above all it is God's, and God can be rather indiscriminating in whom God uses as a means of grace.

11

'You're the man who talks about God': evangelism neither bashful nor cheesy

I am walking down the high street. A small boy from one of the local schools, with mum in tow, sees me and shouts out: 'You're the man who talks about God!' Mum looks very embarrassed. But I smile back. That is who I am, and 'out of the mouths of babes and sucklings . . .'.

This has happened in different parishes on many occasions. And while privately glowing with pride, I am also uncomfortable, because in many other situations I leave God unmentioned. Why?

In this chapter we will reflect on the problem of bashfulness and then go on to think about authentic evangelism in a parochial context. This is not a 'techniques' chapter. Others do that much better than me. It is a 'values for evangelism' chapter.

Bashful

One of my earliest memories is of going to see *Snow White and the Seven Dwarfs*. Apart from falling in love with Snow White, I vividly remember identifying with 'Bashful'. Utterly tongue-tied, clumsily embarrassed, glowing red, with everything feeling like it is going wrong and that everyone is looking. It has dawned on me that I still feel like this, *especially* when I am suddenly invited to share my faith. Why?

Some other vicars are different. I look on with awe at colleagues who can 'gossip the gospel', or make a public Christian
quip in the coffee shop, or naturally lead someone to put their
faith in Christ. But often I shrivel inside and then become
clumsy and inauthentic. Why?

I wonder if it is partly my training. Rightly, theological training requires us to dig up the foundations and check them. It is
important for the welfare of those beyond the visible Church,
let alone our congregations, that we do not send out naive simplistic clergy into ministry. But I worry that it is such a long
journey through theological training on to a *second naïveté*.
One of my former spiritual directors, who is as good and holy
and deep a priest as one could wish for, said to me once that he
could not preach on the Gospels for two years after ordination
because of the legacy of the biblical training he had received.
It had been destructive and disconnected. I think that historical period in the life of the Church is passing. I am not arguing against academically and spiritually rigorous training or
against struggling to put into words complex and challenging
beliefs and experiences – but I do think I ought to be able to
share my faith simply and help others to do that as well.

I wonder if it is partly my role. I am a vicar. Of course I believe in God. Why, therefore, would anyone ask me what
I believe? So I am not often asked. So I am rusty at sharing my
faith. Conversely, when I was an ordinand or a trainer of ordinands, I experienced myself, and watched them, being bom-
barded with questions: 'You are giving up being a police officer/
teacher/nurse etc. to become a priest. Why?' There is something
about that period of transition that people find fascinating. Perhaps in this mode of triggering questions, the dog collar may
be an obstacle to open conversation. The most fun I have had

recently was during a mission when I found a badge, 'I was not always a Christian', and wore it for several days. The shocked faces made me giggle. 'Surely the vicar has always been a Christian!' It provoked lots of conversations, not least with our own church members, many more than did my dog collar.

I wonder also if it is partly the rhythm of our English Anglican church life. Apart from the annual round of confirmation preparation, when do we invite people to take a step of deeper commitment? This partly reflects the Anglican understanding of the spiritual life, of sanctification, as being a slow and lifelong journey, and the deep legacy of the Book of Common Prayer, which assumes regularity rather than crisis. In writing this book I am struck that it is in the area of evangelism that some of our classic texts are at their least helpful, because the context of Classic Anglicanism was so different. It was not that Cranmer, Hooker and Herbert did not recognize the reality of conversion, but their context was overwhelmingly Christian. Conversion was either between 'religions', Protestant and Catholic of course at that time, or what we might call 'renewal', a deepening and enlivening of personal relationship with Christ.

In a context where generation by generation fewer people have faith in Christ, our bashfulness is fatal.

But this bashfulness about evangelism is not inevitable. Some of our Anglican churches do issue regular invitations to commitment, and within living memory parochial missions were commonplace in all traditions of the Church. Perhaps we have gone off the boil more than we recognized.[1] One of the significant achievements of the current round of diocesan-led missions is that it has forced local churches to confront the absence of 'proclamation' in their annual diet.[2] Having said that, one of our curates said after the first weeks of ordained ministry, 'We do mission every week here, don't we?' We do. And in the offer of the love of Christ made at each baptism service or wedding or funeral, we *are* sharing our faith.

That in itself is not without its complications. We are acutely aware of the vulnerability of the bereaved. How tempting to share a confident faith with them. And yet we know that in situations of deep pastoral vulnerability, it is unethical to push a faith solution that the bereaved, when in a stronger place, might reject. And in all our main pastoral contacts there is a power dynamic: 'After all, perhaps the vicar might say no.' So people assent to what we say, often. Real conversation, genuine faith-sharing, is more difficult.

There is another twist. We are, as per William Temple's infamous aphorism, 'the only institution that exists for the benefits of its non-members'.[3] This is both entirely Christ-like in its open-handed generosity but can slip into a sort of *noblesse oblige*. We offer loving acts of service. This is good. It is right that these do not feel linked to a response. This be-devilled much Victorian social action, when a response of grateful faith was expected and too often enforced. So we do not force faith conversations on to those in our debt. Ethics again.[4] But perhaps the most loving gift we could give is to point to Christ. Yet so often I don't. I am caught up in a com-plex of giving and serving from a position of superiority, so I am squeamish about sharing my faith. And occasionally – God forgive me – I wonder if I am assuming that the other person will not be able to make a response of faith.

It was only as I took a break from parish ministry that I realized how tired I was. Part of the fatigue was being the in-strument of the offer of faith most weeks, frequently in an oc-casional office, and most weeks the offer did not produce an instant positive response. I felt as if I had been sharing Christ's love and it had not quite been received. That had left me spiritually very tired; left me prone to unreflective bashfulness. If I did not take time away to be renewed in my passion for Christ, then I was left with a grey love from my side. And that is not a lively place from which to speak of faith.

So how can vicars – and their churches – become less bashful?

Parochial evangelism

One of the stimulating challenges to traditional understandings of ordained ministry has been the work of John Collins on the nature of the diaconate.[5] While I find it spiritually uncomfortable to consider the suggestion that the 'deacon' is not primarily a servant, because this has been such a deep place of spiritual self-understanding for me and other clergy (and I am not entirely convinced by his thesis), nonetheless the new emphasis on the diaconate as 'heralds of Christ's kingdom', proclaiming the gospel in 'word and deed' alongside the classic ministry of the priest as a 'messenger', reaffirms that the work of sharing the faith, of evangelism, is a central task of the parish clergy.[6] How is this to be done?

The C of E has had many evangelists, including among its parish clergy – and it would be worth reflecting on why the reality and value of this ministry has been forgotten in so many sections of the Church. Interestingly, though, when we invite Durham Clergy to analyse their vocations using the APEST typology, many more, to their own surprise, self-describe as 'evangelists'. Perhaps our Church and training has suppressed this charism.

I want to suggest that the main way in which English people relate to their Anglican parish clergy is as pastors. The dominant imagery in the Prayer Book is of the priest as shepherd who is tending to his sheep, *even* when they are lost 'in this naughty world'. It is imagery of recovery. And while, in particular, some of our eighteenth- and nineteenth-century forebears conducted much direct evangelism, their ideal was to restore people to their proper relationship to their Church. We have already had occasion to consider the extraordinary work of William Allen in Bermondsey in the 1880s, baptizing 100 children in one day, but the aim was to make his parish Christian, in that the people related to the Church as the provider of sacrament and teaching. It is essentially, even for this fiery Evangelical, a pastoral relationship.

As a vicar, the overwhelming majority of my encounters with people in our parishes were pastoral, often directly through an occasional office but also in general pastoral care and in contact through community organizations. The most important quality non-churchgoers and churchgoers alike look for in their clergy is authentic compassion. If this is the case, how is evangelism to take place? As we have noted, evangelism is properly constrained in situations of pastoral vulnerability. We do not evangelize the bereaved. We do not proselytize in school. If we do not work pastorally, we will cause offence, even suspicion. Perhaps this is why so many of the new church plants consciously and unconsciously sit light to traditional parish ministry, because it is recognized to be properly constraining. Is it easier to evangelize people where there is no pastoral agenda? That can apply in fluid urban situations, but in settled communities, where the Church has not lost its role of providing spiritual pastoral care, well-conducted occasional offices are an essential prerequisite for evangelism. No fresh expression will flourish in a pit village where funerals are treated with indifference. And we have already noted that much of England is still relatively 'settled'.

So how might 'inherited church' do evangelism? In the parishes where I have served we have tried many things over the last quarter of a century – 'Good News Down Your Street', classic cold-calling door-knocking, prayer visiting, 'soft' events, directly evangelistic events, Alpha, 'Back to Church Sunday', Cafe Church, diocesan episcopal mission – and all had merits, especially in 'breaking up the ground' and moving relationships on, and sometimes in new-found faith. But still the most fruitful methods of 'recruitment' were the occasional offices.

Well-delivered baptism ministry, with sufficient but not excessive preparation, appropriate accessible services and, above all, realistic next steps (that is, a Toddlers Group or All-Age Service not a Sung Eucharist), provides a gentle mechanism for engagement. Ditto with bereavement ministry, including good pre- and post-funeral ministry, excellent funeral services and also memorial services. (But we have to acknowledge, with shame, that too many vicars have lost their commitment and deliver rushed, thin or even shoddy occasional offices. During one funeral visit I was grilled by the family about how long the service would take at the crematorium. In the end, I had to ask why they were asking. It transpired that the last vicar had conducted a family funeral in 12 minutes from beginning to end. How have we lost our sense of priorities as vicars that the dying and the dead and the bereaved are not at the top of the priority list?) Weddings feel more like an investment in the distant future and for someone else, as so many of the couples are not local; even so, good ministry here can produce new church members.

We have seen some specific new initiatives work. Messy Church-style services can be very attractive,[7] especially to the hard-to-reach young families. In our context, 'feeding the bairns' connects deeply with our host communities, as it is about valuing the children generously as well as actually feeding some hungry children. Good-quality schools and youth work also provided the opportunity for amazing conversations and a steady stream of confirmands.

Inherited church is evangelistic when it does inherited church well, when it works creatively with its givens. The role of the vicar is to lead and enable inherited churches to be appropriately evangelistic. To do this, the local church and vicar need to be authentic. In situations where relationship is built over years, then consistency and honesty is the key. Sloganizing is positively harmful in such a context. And that includes parachuting evangelism into settled communities. Fresh voices are invaluable but, in poorer urban contexts and in rural situations, trust is the key bridge. Evangelism is as incarnational a ministry as any.

None of the initiatives we deployed produced spectacular numerical growth, though they did generate new church members. As I think back, I am struck by three inhibiting factors. First, no matter what good events we put on, if the host church was not a place of welcome and spiritual life, then it was hopeless. As a deacon, I was invited back to theological college to share some experiences and reflections on parochial mission. My main reflection – rather pompously – was that we had to see the local church 'converted' first! It was, I fear, true, and in a much harsher climate now, disputatious and cold local churches are doomed.

Second, there is a season in the spiritual life.[8] It just is the case that for certain periods in their lives, people are open to spiritual movement. And if they do not make the move during that period, they will shut down again and the opportunity may be lost. I carry the regret of opportunities lost, people lost. And indeed of those who seemed to find faith but then drifted away. The parable of the sower is surely the parable for the parish clergy. Without being manipulative, this is where the vicar being alive and alert spiritually is crucial. Do we make the visit, speak the word, offer the invitation at the right time, and how do we defend the space to be like this, with so many other pressures crowding in?

The third inhibiting factor was me. Because as vicar I was such a crucial part of the outward-looking face of the Church,[9] when I was over-busy and over-tired, or distracted, then the evangelistic cutting edge of the Church was blunted. This became most evident to me when a new colleague arrived. Why is it that so often it is our curates who receive the compliments – 'That was a lovely service, thank you' – when the incumbents may not? Is it that they bring a freshness and a hope that has been worn out of the longer-serving clergy?

What does it mean to be saved?

Most deeply of all is the question rarely asked: 'What does it mean to be saved?' For some churches, conversion, 'salvation from' future punishment, remains central and has spiritual power. But for most of our English Anglican churches, where we speak the language not of Christian and non-Christian but rather of churchgoer and non-churchgoer, what is our gospel? What are we 'selling'?

Are we 'selling' relationship with God in Christ? Are we selling spiritual, personal and communal transformation in and by Christ? Are we selling membership of loving and transforming community, but which still sees itself very much as part of its host community? Yes! But this is not quite the same as the rather bashful duty, service and habit-shaped Christianity so typical of previous generations of English

Anglicans. The vicar is probably the key instrument of the cultural change from the 1950s to now.

Having ministered in the North-East for thirty years now, I am deeply impressed by the determined faithfulness of our older congregations. 'Faithful' is a word with deep resonances in County Durham, it being the regimental nickname of the Durham Light Infantry, the 'old faithfuls'. It is heroic to be faithful in eviscerated communities where so few voluntary institutions have been able to survive, to be faithful in sustaining sacred places where the deep rites of passage can still be undergone, Christianly.

But often bashfully faithful. There is a proper reticence, suspicion indeed, of verbally slick forms of evangelism. There is something deeply Anglican about this sensibility of 'reserve'. To talk of faith is to walk on holy ground and it is not to be undertaken casually. But it can be done naturally. And where we have failed to facilitate the spiritual and teaching life of a local church – where Christians are enabled to have a lively personal faith and so to speak naturally of the things of God – then we have failed as the very pastors, shepherd-teachers, that we long to be. We have left our churches ill-equipped to be self-sustaining, outward-looking, communicative.

I say 'we' because the joy and the burden of parochial priesthood is to be the leader, pastor, teacher who helps to shape the vision, to set the tone, to do the detailed donkey work, to fight the battles, to heal the wounds. I can only speak about 'inherited churches', but if they are to be effectively evangelistic, then so much else has to be healthy. Vicaring is always a holistic task. Healthy evangelism flows from healthy churches.

A final thought: in Chapter 15 we will reflect on the privilege of being disciples of Jesus. Evangelism is just introducing people to him. Who needs to be bashful about that?

Part 3

WHAT SORTS OF PEOPLE ARE VICARS?

12

Self-fulfilment or self-sacrifice or self-fulfilment?

I was sitting on the Pay Review Committee at school. I was silently grateful that my stipend as a vicar is not widely known. We were appointing teachers at pay levels that were making me giddy. Yes, I know that vicars get a decent non-contributory pension, a detached four-bed house to live in, good working expenses and a helpful tax regime, and that I have been better paid and housed than most people in most of the parishes where I have served. But – it all became very sharp when we needed to buy a house on the basis of a northern vicar's stipend. Should I care? I am not in this for the money. If you meet me in person, you will notice that I am a bit under-dressed (see 'Theology of the cardigan' in Chapter 14). But even so, I have several times lived in one of the biggest houses in the area and certainly with the biggest garden. And I get to wear the fanciest clothes in the parish.

This chapter begins the section of the book when we reflect on the 'character' of the vicar, and this particular chapter may feel like a roller coaster. We will start by reflecting on the self-fulfilment that goes with being a vicar. Then we will honestly face the cost and ask: 'Is this kind of self-sacrifice appropriate?' We will finish by reflecting on what is Christian fulfilment anyway.

Being looked up to as a vicar

I had been seated at the top table at a Cambridge college. I found myself sitting between three international bankers. They were old friends and we were having a convivial chat. I kept a poker face as they lamented the hard time they had been having as international bankers. They then asked me what I was up to. I explained I was a northern vicar. There was a sort of bemused but respectful silence as if they had met a bearded explorer who had just emerged from the frozen wasteland. I don't think that I am over-reading the conversation to note that respect. And despite the loss of status of vicars, which is of course real and tangible, it is still my experience that I – and I see this in my vicar colleagues – am treated with respect by those with whom we work. Being a vicar is still a relatively high-status occupation, despite the corrosive impact of how the Church has handled the scandal of child sexual abuse. And I have been struck, working with journalists, that while they regard us as a bit strange (we appear still to believe in God!), they come with an assumption that we know our communities well enough to speak publicly for them and that we are essentially doing good, sometimes remarkable good, locally.

Vicars talk ideas and values. We are on the whole a reasonably well-educated type of person. We are committed by our ordination vows to care for the marginalized and vulnerable. We are called to be peacemakers. We are trusted, indeed expected to speak the language of 'love and justice' in public in ways that few others are, without cynicism. So we are (mostly) seen as valuable on school governing bodies or as trustees. We are trusted with 'big stuff'. The deputy head at a local community school was tragically killed in a car accident. The vicar was asked to 'MC' the memorial service. A local free school was forced to close. The vicar was asked to host the closing service. A new war memorial was erected. The vicar was asked to bless it. Some houses were damaged by fire in a village. The vicar and local church were trusted with the informal money collection. A new funeral director starts up. The vicar is asked to bless the viewing rooms. Every vicar can add their events to this list. If I walk the street wearing a dog collar, I get natural smiles. And I appear to have a calming effect on irate parents and naughty children! There is much about being a vicar that enhances self-esteem.

All of this runs in an odd relationship to language of 'professionalism'. Some parochial clergy delight in rubbishing the word 'professional'. It is felt to be unchristian and to distance the clergy from the laity. Further, there is a worry among some that 'professionalism' really means 'priestcraft' and is thus unacceptable to them theologically. And there is the reality for vicars that we are generalists. Few working weeks enabled me to prioritize my core gifts as I would have liked. I might be bouncing between failed church boilers, endless meetings and occasional-office visits. Where was I an expert? But I want to celebrate this word 'professional'. It speaks to me about high and accountable standards; about some sense that I do know what I am doing; that others expect me to know what I am doing and to do it properly; that I have been trained to do this and am accountable in the doing of it. Francis Bridger writes wisely and theologically on this issue:

criticism that guidelines amount to an unwarranted concession to managerialism must be seen as misplaced. They simply set out what it means to act in a manner consistent with a calling to ministry and should be seen as an attempt to work out in concrete terms the practice of vocation in a contemporary setting. As a result, 'profession', in a clergy context, must be seen as possessing not one meaning but two: on one hand to describe the sociological reality of a group of people who operate according to conventions and practices developed by the group; and on the other, as an indication that this group stands for – professes – a set of transcendent values and principles which derive from a theology of vocation.[1]

Historically, English Anglican clergy have not always been noted for their professionalism.[2] I hope we are not seen as 'amateurs' now.

Of course, there is a downside. I have deliberately not cited opinion poll surveys because two of the more recent polls suggest either that 'priests are less trusted than the average person in the street' or that 'priests are in the top five most trusted types of people'. That there has been an understandable loss of trust in the Church as institution is undeniable. This is aggravated by the reality and the narrative of church decline. Because our livelihood and vocation is so tied up with the 'success' of the institution of the Church, the constant rhetoric in the public domain of decline (irrelevance) is wearing. Much more so is the reality of increasing pressure on vicars as their numbers are reduced and workload increases. Clergy morale can be fragile. It is not surprising that the C of E has convened a task force to consider the urgent issue of clergy well-being.[3]

There is another odd dynamic in this conversation about the status of vicars. We have all seen the 'Old Rectory': either the eighteenth-century one, which was the fruit of clergy wealth during the Agricultural Revolution, or the nineteenth-century one, which was the fruit of clergy wealth during the Industrial Revolution. Status indeed! It was the case that in the poorer Victorian parishes the only people living locally who had servants were the vicar and the doctor. (That is why Victorian clergy built vicarages with many bedrooms, including attics with backstairs for the servants.) I for one am glad that we have lost this status. Victorian clergy would often publish accounts of their lengthy holidays in their parish magazines. I wonder how this was received by those who could count their holidays on the finger of one hand? How did the vicar who described the dockers in his parish as 'utter brutes' work effectively with them to share the love of Christ? Why were Victorian clergy so often social and political authority figures in their communities? Did this help the growth of the kingdom of God? It was a clergyman magistrate who ordered the charge of the yeomanry at Peterloo. We thank God now for the example of vicars who fought for the liberation of their parishioners. But wealth and status was an obstacle to the mission of the Church. It is better that we are (relatively) poorer now.

But the cost

To my deep embarrassment, I was interviewed by two national newspapers about clergy stress.[4] It forced me to examine wherein lay the stress. Of course, not all stress is bad. And I worked alongside other people who were sometimes dangerously stressed. I think again of our head teachers, who had to cope with both the stress of complex and conflict-filled roles and also the threat of inspection, which could destroy their careers. I think of the GP who said to me with some wonderment, 'I can only cope with working four days a week. How do you keep going?' But I preferred my six-day to his four-day week. Or I think of those whose lives were stressed because of illness and bereavement, the addictions of family members, crowded houses, bad neighbours and money shortages – with no prospect of escape. That is toxic stress. So I had to try to define clergy stress more precisely. I noted four things that were distinctive.

First, many vicars still live on the patch. I remember in one parish feeling sick every time we drove home from holiday towards the parsonage: 'Will we have been burgled this time?' Feeling under siege in one's home is a very exhausting experience. Few other professionals now live in poor parishes. There is a unique wear and tear about living in a place that feels unloved: ugly graffiti, broken bottles and shabby housing. Of course this only applies to a proportion of our vicars, but many of us still live in publicly recognized houses. People know where to find us, and often at inconvenient times of the day and night. The phone I can ignore, but not the front door. It is not surprising that the 'Experiences of Ministry' survey recorded the high level of impact on vicarage families just of being vicarage families.

Clergy partners themselves were surveyed and, while broadly positive about their own experience, they did report making regular sacrifices for their partner's role, and more than half (57%) agreed that they did not know where their partner's ministry ended and family life began.[5]

It is good that the draft Clergy Covenant addresses the pressures of living a public life in a publicly known house explicitly:

Given the public nature of elements of the work of the ordained minister, the support and encouragement of those who share their intimate lives with ordained ministers is a significant contribution to their care and wellbeing. This is particularly true when ordained ministers inhabit a home associated with a particular cure or ministerial post. It is therefore part of the responsibility of the whole church to provide for the minister's household.[6]

Second, as the wife of one of my fellow vicars put it, 'You are the only people who are required to wear your faith on your sleeves.' Irrespective of how a vicar feels about God, she is required to say public prayers and to offer spiritual care. I can often remember standing at the stall in the crematorium as I was about to press the button that sent the body to the furnace and wondering, 'What do I really believe now?' This is not the same as proper professional self-care. After my father died, with support from my colleagues, I had some time away from funeral ministry. But often in the bumps of life and ministry, we can find ourselves wrestling with, or seemingly distant from, God. This cannot often be shared because it becomes a distraction for those for whom we are caring. Again vicars are not alone in this tension, but because faith is such an existential reality, doubt is something we have to manage professionally – but at a cost. And, of course, when the C of E is embarrassing or worse, we can distance ourselves from it only a little.

I had led a school Eucharist on St Hild and celebrated the breadth of her ministry. My point had been, 'Look what St Hild did for God. What could you do for God?' That night General Synod voted against the proposal to consecrate women to the episcopate. I walked into school the following morning. The head teacher greeted me with a raised eyebrow: 'I thought you had said to the children we could do anything for God?' I was duly embarrassed and indeed angry.

The third pressure is the complexity of the task, especially with multiple responsibilities and feeling like I never achieved my goals. An image had come to me. Each week I imagined myself setting out on a sailing boat heading towards a point on a distant island. Most weeks I ended up just avoiding the rocks on the nearby shore where I had been blown back by wind and wave. I thought this was my own inadequacy until I shared this image with other more senior incumbents who nodded gravely and said this was their experience too. We have already noted that the 'Experiences of Ministry' survey identified that many vicars were spending much time on tasks for which they felt ill-equipped and which were, in fact, wearing them down, especially administration. There are few vicars for whom this is not a frustration. Another finding was that multiple churches added exponentially to the complexity, sense of distraction and administrative burden.

> Incumbents whose ministries span multiple contexts felt less in control of their daily and weekly schedule than those in a single church setting, a finding that was especially pronounced for those in rural settings. This meant that many desirable activities such as outreach and pastoral care could become squeezed out of their weeks.[7]

As most vicars now have multiple churches, most vicars are experiencing this.

The fourth distinctive characteristic was isolation. We have already noted the internal dynamics of isolation – 'I can and should be able to do this on my own' – but we should also note the structural dynamics. As a vicar there are some confidences that cannot be shared locally. Especially in rural ministry, the next vicar or fellow minister might be miles away. We know that clerical isolation is damaging and that it can become self-reinforcing, especially if it is linked to feelings of failure, shame and depression. Few other professionals would now work in isolation.

I was chatting with one of our new incumbents, someone who had succeeded in demanding professional jobs in the health service and industry. She said to me: 'I have never been as stretched as I have been in the first year of incumbency.' That statement has haunted me. As I sit with our new incumbents year by year and watch them shoulder much more complex pastoral charges than were the norm a generation ago, I fear for them and for their families. There is a level of personal and family cost about being a vicar that is genuinely frightening.

Self-sacrifice

Should we be expecting this level of self- (and family) sacrifice? My first response is 'of course not', 'especially not our families'. But I want to recognize that the call to ministry is costly. Pastoral ministry – vicaring – is cross-shaped. We live with confidence in the resurrection and all that is to come, but we live in the 'not yet'.[8] We walk with those and as those still subject to human frailty, mortality and sin. As with Christ's own ministry, we see glimpses of the kingdom of God but we also find ourselves sitting with those whose bodies and hearts are breaking and whose time here on earth is coming to an end. Pastoral ministry preserves us from spiritual fantasy. In the next chapter, we will return to the question of the mood and mode of being of vicars, but I want to name here the emotional and spiritual cost of vicaring. The word I used and that I hear frequently is 'relentless'. Just when we are at our most exhausted, another crisis erupts. Because that is the human condition. I look in the faces of our vicars and I see care lines, from loving relentlessly. This is self-sacrifice.

I think we need to name the cost of vicaring. Both for reasons of honesty – this is what it is like – and also so that we equip ourselves spiritually and practically for reality. If we go into vicaring expecting spacious continuous joy, we will be in for a nasty surprise. Our liturgy teaches us this. The model is the Good Shepherd, and while we do not see Jesus as glum, nor can we ignore the cost to him of his relentless loving. We are people who have taken up our cross to follow one who died on a cross. We are to grow into the likeness of Christ. The imagery is of 'living sacrifice'. Because our foundational ordination is as deacons, we are therefore those who give their lives in service, in imitation of the one who washed filthy feet. It is not surprising that a key moment in the ordination service is when the bishop says to the ordinand: 'You cannot bear the weight of this calling in your own strength, but only by the grace and power of God.'[9]

This is hard fact.

The Book of Common Prayer is unsurprisingly tougher. So the Collect reminds the deacons of the example of St Stephen. The imagery overwhelmingly is of service. For priests, the Gospel reading is John 10, the good shepherd who lays down his life for the sheep. As well as the language of dignity and authority, the priest should 'never cease your labour, your care and diligence, until you have done all that lieth in you, according to your bounden duty'. This feels daunting and exhausting but many clergy internalize this deeply. I can picture the new deacons and priests and vicars as they lie or kneel on the chancel steps, giving their all to Christ. Vicars make the sacrifice of their freedom to serve Christ in his world and in his people. I do not want to minimize the extent and seriousness of this call. I do not want to lose this fire in my belly or in the bellies of my fellow vicars: 'never cease your labour, your bounden duty'.

Am I a doormat, then?

The young GP looked at me and said, 'If you go under, you are no use to anyone, let alone yourself. You have to take care of yourself.' The language of self-sacrifice needs careful moderation.

We have already had occasion to touch on the fantasy of 'I am Jesus'. We are not. And there is spiritual pride here as well as fantasy. I can overestimate my capacity – energy, wisdom, time, health – to tackle an issue and imagine I am Superman. We have noted earlier the perils of TINA ('there is no alternative'), especially when it means I, the vicar, have to be the one who does this task. Modern clergy training is much more up-front about being honest about our need to be needed and the risks of compulsive behaviour. This is now part of our working practices.

> The clergy should be aware of the dangers of dependency in pastoral relationships. Manipulation, competitiveness or collusion on either side of the pastoral encounter should be avoided. Self-awareness should be part of the relationship. The responsibility for maintaining appropriate boundaries always rests with the clergy.[10]

Like most vicars, I am an introvert. So I should not pretend that I can manage limitless public engagements without needing space to recharge. Part of the discipline of being a professional is precisely not over-engaging emotionally so that we can manage in demanding situations, to the point of being able to withdraw ourselves when we know we are out of our depth or no longer safe. 'The clergy should discern and acknowledge their own limitations of time, competence and skill. They will need to seek support, help and appropriate training and, on occasion, to refer to specialist agencies.'[11]

So there are healthy boundaries to self-giving. There is also appropriate self-care. In spiritual direction, we are often reminded that Jesus said, 'Love your neighbour as you love *yourself*', the implication being that we should at least love ourselves as we love our neighbours. It is so much easier to see in others when they are not caring for themselves properly. But am *I* taking regular time out and time off? Am I nurturing family and friends? Am I allowing myself to be held accountable? Am I being refreshed as me? Am I being renewed spiritually or do I imagine I can go on without God? Am I taking care of 'Brother Ass' (St Francis' harsh but revealing description of his own body)? So that there is no pretence, I can answer all these rhetorical questions by saying 'no'. The question for me then is 'Why?' Sometimes the truthful answer is 'events' and sometimes it is 'structures', but more often I think it is pride and anxiety. That is a spiritual and emotional issue and a professional one.[12]

And of course vicars are not doormats.

As we noted earlier, sometimes as the sole professional in the team the vicar might be the one who puts the chairs out or puts them away. There is wisdom in the old saying, 'Beware the curate who won't move the chairs.' (However, it drives deep change when the curate can't put the chairs out. I served with a priest who was increasingly confined to a wheelchair. This liberated the church for team working in a way that a fit young curate would never have achieved.) But I do hear too frequently of vicars who are dumped on with numerous tasks and who are left exhausted. There is a toxic lay emotional response to the language of servanthood that assumes the vicar is a slave to the congregation. This needs naming and challenging whenever and wherever it happens.

Several years ago I was leading a retreat for clergy from a neighbouring diocese. I entitled one of the sessions, 'Bruises I have left and bruises I am still carrying'. My idea was to allow the clergy to own mistakes and perhaps get something off their chests if they had been hurt. There was indeed some reflection on the first half of this topic but I was hit by a tidal wave of hurt. As a retreat director I am used to time-tabling one-to-one sessions. On this retreat I had to arrange to meet after dinner, first thing in the morning, whenever there was a gap, all the clergy who needed to come and offload excruciating experiences of being hurt by their flock. I found it hard to hear the stories: of expenses held back as a blackmailing tool; of vicars returning from leave to find their churches had been (illegally) altered; of flat refusal of mission opportunities; of shouting matches, vicars openly insulted at church councils; of stony silences; of bullying. I must note that I heard many fewer stories from the clergy about the bruises they had left. I hear about them from lay people, and I have left some bruises myself. I know this happens. But I was shocked then – but am no longer – by these accounts of the wilful undermining of the leadership and person of the vicar. The worst case I heard of was when a very effective young (celibate) gay priest was driven out of his church by homophobic bullying. Institution-ally, the C of E lacks mechanisms for dealing with this sort of lay bullying. Conflict is endemic to the human condition: bullying does not have to be. In these circumstances, leader-ship is crucifying. No wonder some vicars shy away from it or break under its weight.

But vicars sometimes have to be shit-shovellers. I had come out of the back gate of our vicarage and was heading to church when a disgusting smell hit my nose. I explored. On the steps of the church hall was a pile of human faeces. I could not and would not leave this for someone else to deal with. There fol-lowed a rather gruesome exercise of cleaning. I used the ex-perience as the basis for my next theological reflection: 'The priest as shit-shoveller!' It reflected, I realize now, the fact that I was going through a demanding patch in ministry and this felt like the last straw. Our lay church members would have done exactly what I did. Shit-shovelling is not a uniquely vicarly ministry. But it is part of vicaring, both as fact and as meta-phor. What do we think Jesus washed off his disciples' feet?

Self-fulfilment

That deeply unpleasant image is a good place to start this last section. Is vicaring fulfilling? Not always! But often. Despite all the above, vicars still regularly come out near the top of the job satisfaction surveys.[13] The fulfilment lies both in the service of Christ and also in serving Christ in those who come to his Church for help. There is much joy in vicaring.

It would be an odd ministry that offered 'life in all its full-ness' but that reduced its servants to exhausted ill-health. If vicars embody only 'cost' then this is a contradiction to their deepest calling. There is a pragmatic and, much more deeply, a missional reason for clergy well-being. Are we good examples of what it is to be a disciple of Christ – or terrifying warnings?

There is a deeper joy. We were taking part in a day on Ignatian spirituality for the parish clergy. For one exercise, we were invited to think back over our clerical working lives and how we felt about each role. I know this is different for different people – we live in a fallible Church – but I was able to celebrate that each post I had held had been overwhelmingly life-giving. I contrasted that with the drudgery of much working life, and I was grateful. I was also moved that I had been enabled to flourish as me in each of those roles.

I want to finish by quoting from a homily given by Bishop Mark Bryant, then Bishop of Jarrow, at an ordination retreat (reproduced with permission):

Many years ago, I worked with a priest who had trained at St Stephen's House over 50 years ago. And Stephen would often tell the story how, on the first night at St Stephen's House, the principal summoned the new boys into the chapel. And he said to them, 'I wonder why you think God has called you to be priests? You may think that you will be able to preach fine sermons, you may think that you will be a great pastor, you may think that you will be able to say Mass rather beautifully. But has it ever occurred to you that God may have chosen to give you the gift of the ordained priesthood because that is the only way that he can save your immortal soul?'

I heard Stephen tell that story a number of times and, if I am absolutely honest, I think I have only come to understand it in the last 15 years or so. Because what I think I understand that college principal all those years ago to be saying is that God has given me the gift of the diaconate and the priesthood and rather strangely the gift of being a bishop because God has worked out that that is the only way he can help me to be the person who he has truly made me to be.

And therefore I wonder if indeed God has called you to be deacons and priests in his Church because that is the only way that he can help each one of you to become fully the wonderful person he made you to be.

I think that may be true for me. In which case, self-sacrifice is truly self-fulfilment. This is one of the deep principles of Christianity for all Christians.

Then he said to them all, 'If any want to become my followers, let them deny themselves and take up their cross daily and follow me. For those who want to save their life will lose it, and those who lose their life for my sake will save it.
(Luke 9.23–24)

It may be a special gift for the ordained.

13

Are vicars sad?

How often do you weep as a vicar? When we were training ordinands and curates for funeral ministry, one of the disciplines we passed on was: 'Weep before and weep after the funeral, but do not weep during the funeral.' But I have often had to bite the inside of my cheek during a funeral, or sit with moist eyes in a home or at a bedside. It is not just the obviously tragic cases – the lost babies, the young suicides, the traffic accidents, the military funerals – but it can be the old widower who has lost his wife after sixty years and looks utterly bewildered by loss, or the funeral with half a dozen mourners because someone's life has contracted so much. I have shed many tears as a vicar. As we should. We 'weep with those who weep'. But should vicars be 'sad'? Or perhaps 'solemn' is a different way of putting it. The question comes from George Herbert, who described a mostly serious demeanour for vicars. Is this the right tone for us to adopt – 'The man in black'?

We will also in this chapter explore an alternative modern definition of 'sad'. Urban slang would define this as 'of poor quality', 'displeasing', or worst of all, 'uncool'. So should vicars be 'cool' if we are to commend Christ in our culture? Or not? Are vicars counter-cultural in their very strangeness? To put it another way, what does it mean to be a 'fool for Christ' in our generation?

'The Parson in mirth'

Herbert devoted a short chapter to this question. He wrote:

> The Country Parson is generally sad, because he knows
> nothing but the Cross of Christ, his mind being defixed
> on it with those nails wherewith his Master was; or if he
> have any leisure to look from thence, he meets continually
> with two most sad spectacles, Sin and Misery; God
> dishonoured every day, and man afflicted. Nevertheless,
> he sometimes refresheth himself, as knowing that nature
> will not bear everlasting droopings, and that pleasantness
> of disposition is a great key to do good; not only because all
> men shun the company of perpetual severity, but also for
> that when they are in company, instructions seasoned with
> pleasantness both enter sooner and root deeper. Wherefore
> he condescends to human frailties both in himself and
> others, and intermingles some mirth in his discourses
> occasionally, according to the pulse of the hearer.[1]

I don't think of Herbert as a killjoy,[2] but I do think that this
mood of seriousness was one that was held up as the model of
priestly living for centuries. The task of the vicar was to bring
people to salvation. This is not a light task. Because the human
condition is one of sin, the role of the vicar is to embody the
fear of punishment and the hope for redemption. We are back
in a world of social and religious authority utterly alien to our
world now, a world where even laughter was regarded as a distraction from the work of the priest.[3] And notice how Herbert
seems to be straining against his own nature. He recognized
that 'perpetual severity' was off-putting and depressing and
that a little light humour aided communication. But up until

a couple of generations ago (my childhood), all vicars wore black, the colour of severity and mourning. Vicars were 'sad'. Should they be?

This may seem an irrelevant question now when we can buy a multitude of brightly coloured clerical shirts, blouses or dresses – if we wear clerical dress at all. And I think our culture expects its vicars to be cheerful and friendly, for complex reasons, which Andrew Rumsey explores:

> Especially when adorned with clerical collar, the parish priest is by definition approachable. If he or she were to respond to the myriad 'neighbourly' approaches from parishioners in an aggressive or ignorant manner, 'alarm signals' denoting the breaking of an unspoken social contract would be quick to follow. For better or for worse, the priest embodies the neighbourly ethics of the parish – they are expected to act, as it were, 'parochially'.[4]

This may be why grumpy vicars are doing much more damage than they realize.

Behind this lurks a deep theological question. What is the condition of the world? And, therefore, how urgent is the task? How dominant is the pain? In our role as prophets and messengers, are we here primarily to warn and to mourn – 'the woman in black'?

The joy perspective

We were celebrating our patronal festival with sung evensong. One of our new members was a Charismatic from a Nonconformist background. She had never experienced the solemnity of evensong before. She came to me in some distress at the end of the service. 'What do you mean by calling me a miserable offender? My heavenly Father loves me!' It was a little sign of how much Evangelicalism has changed in the past two generations, but this brief exchange also invites us to ponder honestly how and why our presentation of the gospel may have changed since the sixteenth century.

I wrote earlier that I think and experience pastoral ministry as more cross- than resurrection-shaped. But I want to contrast this paradoxically with the joy that infuses Christian life and therefore ministry: not primarily a joy in the glory that is to come, but joy in the love and grace experienced now within the beauty of the gift of creation.

Despite the experience of my Nonconformist sister, I think Thomas Cranmer was a liturgist primarily of grace.[5] He had experienced the forgiveness of God himself and his liturgy speaks of the passionate love of God for relationship with humankind.

And to the end that we should always remember the exceeding great love of our Master and only Saviour Jesus Christ, thus dying for us, and the innumerable benefits which by his precious blood-shedding he hath obtained to us; he hath instituted and ordained holy mysteries, as pledges of his love, and for a continual remembrance of his death, to our great and endless comfort.[6]

God wants all to be saved – 'who desireth not the death of a sinner, but rather that he may turn from his wickedness and live'.[7] But Cranmer's liturgy is shaped by his theological world view that all humankind is properly under the judgement of God and therefore the task of the Church is to save some. Thus the work of proclamation is first warning and then the offer of grace. Is this a 'black preaching scarf' task?

We find in Hooker, and much more explicitly in Herbert, a conviction of the passionate grace of God that constantly reaches out to humankind with the offer of love, forgiveness and new life. Is this a 'white stole' task? I want to argue strongly that we need to embrace our own development as Anglicans to a soteriology that stresses the priority of grace, where judgement is not abolished but held in its proper place, of reserve. Therefore the proper mood of the vicar is warm, open welcome – 'over-acceptance', to quote Sam Wells.[8] This requires at least a smile.

But it is hard to sustain. All vicars carry the bruises of relationships that go nowhere; for example, the many baptism preparation meetings with families after which we do not see them again. I do not think the right response to this is either legalism or shoddiness, but it is hard to sustain this depth of welcome if it is not rooted in a living spirituality of grace and gratitude. One of the best of the innovations in the modern ordination liturgies is the naming of the candidates. So, as well as the general sense that God in Christ calls people to be deacons and priests, the Church now affirms that *N* specifically has been called to be a priest. As well as the many prayers for what they will do, they are surrounded by prayer reminding them of what God in Christ has done and is doing *in calling them*. Perhaps we might weave more of this affirmation of calling into our Chrism Eucharists so we are reminded of the assurance of our call, as well as renewing our promise to follow.

Herbert, as so often, expresses the life-giving quality of the call in beautiful monosyllables:

Come, my Way, my Truth, my Life:
Such a Way, as gives us breath:
Such a Truth, as ends all strife:
Such a Life, as killeth death.

. . .

Come, my Joy, my Love, my Heart:
Such a Joy, as none can move:
Such a Love, as none can part:
Such a Heart, as joys in love.[9]

The security of this invitation comes in the experience of relationship with Christ, though Herbert also reminds us there is much affliction and struggle in this relationship.[10] It is rooted in profound experience of the love of Christ embodied on the cross – back to cross-shaped ministry. Herbert links this exquisitely to communion:

Love is that liquor sweet and most
    divine,
Which my God feels as blood; but I, as
    wine.[11]

It is both the peril and the privilege of priesthood that this reality can be routinized.

I wonder if alongside this biblical, liturgical, spiritual, Eucharistic locus of encounter with Christ, vicars need to have eyes and ears open for Christ in other people and in creation, so that we experience the whole world as infused with 'the grandeur of God'.[12] Some days it is as if we meet God in

Christ everywhere. I think of the welcome and loving faith in the eyes of an old widow, whose first question is, 'How are you?' Or I am picturing the gruff love of a dad, whose wife had died a hard death, trying to comfort his angry sharp-elbowed teenage daughter, and not giving up. Or the brightness of a summer blue sky over children playing in the litter-strewn street, or the gnarled trees striving to bring green life to hot tarmacked pavements. I often wonder if vicars are a little 'mad' when they experience themselves walking in this God-infused world. (I have been mad, so I am allowed to say this.)

Fools for Christ

I am writing this on a day when there is yet another report on the percentage of vicars who have been insulted or even assaulted while serving Christ. This is a 'mad' way of life. Whereas once this was a career with good prospects for the second or third son, now we are entering into a lifetime of demanding service with an 'invisible boss' in a wobbly institution. I look at the young ordinands and my heart aches for them. Do they really know what they are doing? It is 'mad'. 'Better to stay in our secular jobs?' 'No, still better to take the risk with Christ!'

We have lived with such solidity in the C of E for so long that we lose touch with the imagery and reality of Christian ministry as risky. But when the Church has been at its edgiest it has been the experience of its ministers, lay and ordained, that life is not sensible or balanced or predictable. For examples, we could look to the martyrs of the early Church or the Desert Fathers and Mothers, the Celtic saints, the Franciscans, the heroines and heroes of the Reformations, of the great missionary expansion of the Church, or the 'slum priests'. Am I the only vicar to feel the disjunction between reading these narratives and the humdrum nature of our own working days? The Church, including the C of E, has a long history of extreme risk-taking ministers, though it is not our normal rhetoric and imagery. In a time of profound change and challenge, do we need to recover this as our core vision? The vicar as a 'fool for Christ'?

> We are fools for the sake of Christ, but you are wise in Christ. We are weak, but you are strong. You are held in honour, but we in disrepute. To the present hour we are hungry and thirsty, we are poorly clothed and beaten and homeless, and we grow weary from the work of our own hands. When reviled, we bless; when persecuted, we endure; when slandered, we speak kindly. We have become like the rubbish of the world, the dregs of all things, to this very day.
> (1 Corinthians 4.10–13)

Here of course Paul is both angry and also using a rhetorical devise to mock his opponents in Corinth and to shock these Christians into seeing that weakness not strength is the proof of authenticity in Christ. I wonder if this is the deep corruption of Establishment: that we are instinctively looking for security rather than risk, or even weakness, as our tests of the presence of God in Christ?

I was very grateful to be paid a stipend and to live in a provided house and to know that I have a pension. There are issues of justice and of well-being here. I am not suggesting that we de-institutionalize the Church when it comes to employment conditions. But I do wonder if we need both to recognize that in our current context what we ask our vicars to do is a bit 'mad', and also to allow the imagery of unrespectable risk to be more dominant.

The vicar as clown

Henri Nouwen uses a kinder image than madness – the clown.

> Clowns are not in the centre of events. They appear between the great acts, fumble and fall, and make us smile again after the tensions created by the heroes we come to admire. The clowns don't have it together, they do not succeed in what they try to do, they are awkward, out of balance, and left-handed, but . . . they are on our side.[13]

I like this image, which we might apply to the vicar. It is an image that lacks self-importance. I do have some respect for the dignity of my office, but I have done some very silly things as a vicar. I remember shoving a bumble ball up my surplice at a carol service to try to communicate the delirious excitement of knowing that God is in our world with us. I think some disapproved. I especially enjoy being silly in schools, because children laugh. 'Bubble prayers' make me laugh every time. Is it okay to laugh when praying? Sometimes, of course. It is a good test of our vicaring, whether we can be genuinely fun with children.

The clown is also an image of the human condition – clumsy, on the receiving end of 'bad luck', messy. It is perhaps no spiritual coincidence that the fragility of the modern Church is being addressed by Messy Church. Perhaps we have been too 'ordered'. The clown brings a sense of joy in life. Perhaps that is what vicars are supposed to do. Note that the clown is also very professional: well prepared, intentional, not an amateur, not clownish.

Another wounded saint was also drawn to this image of the priest as clown, Jim Cotter. In a prose poem, he reflected on the roles and places of the clown:

> The court jesters who are the only ones allowed to tell the king unpleasant truths, getting away with it because they have no ambition for power, casting doubt on old certainties, ridiculing conventional wisdoms, discovering truths in the absurd.

> Irrepressible fools who bounce back for more, resurrection showing up death for the joke it is, voices merry with the laughter that is our saving grace.

> Entertainers at the Great Banquet. Ah, but wait. At this Feast the King comes down from the throne, for he is himself the clown for his guests – or rather the Clown of clowns, Fool of fools, the only Entertainer of Jesters.[14]

Can we bear to imagine Jesus as a clown? And as our role model in that way?

There is a thread on social media at this very moment – yet another discussion of whether Jesus was funny, or not. When we have to answer this question with weighty articles by heavy-duty biblical scholars, it seems to me that we have lost the point. My test is: children liked Jesus. He liked them. He must have been fun to be with. So, I do not think vicars are sad: serious when needed, passionately committed, but with a smile on their faces, like Jesus had.

14

'Do justice . . . love kindness . . . walk humbly with your God'

We were sitting on a garage forecourt. A clergy colleague who had a sideline in selling cars was helping us to choose a replacement family car. Our colleague had a strong sense that God was guiding us to buy an expensive Volvo. We had a stronger sense that God was not. We bought a Vauxhall instead. On the morning of our first Sunday in the new parish, the car was broken into and the radio stolen. Two weeks later, the night before the radio repair man was due, the car was stolen. We had to phone the nice man and say we had no car in which to put a radio. We did get the car back in the end, with a few dents and holes. And it fitted in with driving round the social housing estates rather better than a Volvo.

The funny sting in the tail was that my first christening in the same parish included beer and sandwiches in a local pub afterwards. It was a pub where we had been told, 'Don't go in The ——, Vicar. It's too rough!' We were chatting over lunch, and the lasses asked us whether we were enjoying settling into the village. We replied, 'Yes, we feel very welcome. Apart from the man who has stolen our car.' They laughed. I thought this was a particularly tough form of Geordie humour. No: they whispered to me that the boyfriend of the young lass sitting next to me was a professional car thief.

I laughed too. He would never have sunk so low as to steal our old Vauxhall!

Let's treat ourselves to a few sweeping generalizations. We live in the UK in a world of illusion: false news; politicians telling bare-faced lies; photo-shopped images of models; people pretending to believe in causes; celebrities weeping tears over disadvantaged children and asking for money when their personal fortunes alone could revolutionize the lives of thousands of these children. And all this accentuated by the bombardment of the social media and the influence of the unseen algorithms. We do not know how to find what is authentic. It is, I suggest, the deep search in our postmodern society. What is authentic – where words and actions match – and thus can be trusted? In this context, what does it mean for the Church, for vicars, to be authentic?

True authenticity

Not all Victorian clergy were wealthy. Until the 1940s, the C of E was a profoundly unequal institution, where neighbouring vicars were paid widely differing amounts of money depending on the endowment of the benefice. I enjoy telling people that the C of E is now one of the most socialist organizations in England, with a very flat pay scale. When I started as a curate, I was paid £1,000 a year less than my highly experienced responsibility-bearing training incumbent. This is one of the C of E's best kept secrets, slightly obscured by bishops living in palaces, though that era too is finally passing.

Why am I beginning this discussion by talking about money? Because our people know, somehow, that Jesus did not have a lot of money and they think the Church should not be wealthy. Money is one of our first tests of authenticity. Wealthy, hypocritical clergy were a scandal in Victorian times.[1]

But the C of E had the social and political power to ride out such challenges (it thought). In fact the Church's use of its wealth has done lasting damage to its mission. In the Durham coalfields or the lead-mining valleys of the Pennines, Methodism was the religion of the people because Anglicanism was the religion of the (oppressive) mine-owners; and often it was the C of E that owned the mine or leased the land. It took the stubborn, costly heroism of a Westcott to change this perception in County Durham.[2] It is no wonder that Jesus talked so much about money. We can be blind and fiercely self-justifying in this area. Marx described religion as the 'opium of the people', within which he included the ability of the bourgeoisie to hide its injustice and cruelty from itself.[3] Perhaps we might learn self-awareness from one of our arch opponents.[4]

We know that we need to read Herbert with a little suspicion – the book is an idealized vision of vicaring, and he had wealth – but he is deeply wise about money:

> because country people live hardly, and therefore, as feeling their own sweat, and consequently knowing the price of money, are offended much with any who by hard usage increase their travail, the country parson is very circumspect in avoiding all covetousness, neither being greedy to get, nor niggardly to keep, nor troubled to lose any worldly wealth; but in all his words and actions slighting and disesteeming it, even to a wondering that the world should so much value wealth, which in the day of wrath, hath not one dram of comfort for us.[5]

This is not one of the purple passages often cited from Herbert, but perhaps it should be. Even though he may only have been

185

a country vicar for three years, he has learned the idiom. So 'country people live hardly' – they work hard and have hard lives – and therefore they know the 'price of money': a tautology or someone who has seen how hard farming folk had to work to earn their pennies. And they would have been ultra-sensitive to someone who increased this travail by hard usage: the vicar might have had glebe land on which he collected a rent, and he would probably have collected his tithes, as he did until the 1930s. A harsh vicar would increase his people's travail. Is Herbert hypocritical or truthful when he writes so beautifully of covetousness in past, present and future tenses? I think not. He gave up the gilded life of court and university for the humility of a country parish.

We are not reading Herbert naively, but as we reflect on his values and how we translate them into the twenty-first century, this wisdom about simple living resonates. Is how we manage our money – modest as it often is – the first sign of authenticity?

The second test of authenticity is compassionate welcome. All vicars will have been on the receiving end of requests, and then pressure and complaints when they do not accede to a particular request for an occasional office. 'But why can't we have the wedding on Boxing Day?' Dealing with the general public can be demanding, as anyone in a service industry will tell us. But there is a deeper level of expectation: that we will be compassionately welcoming because Jesus was kind to people. We may wish to nitpick about Jesus, but our people see more clearly. They know, somehow, that Jesus was not on the side of the religious authorities but on the side of the marginalized. They know that Jesus means love. They expect us to be loving. So my basic rule of thumb as a vicar was to say a big welcoming

'Yes!' Even when it put my own life under pressure (Boxing Day weddings . . .). Especially in working-class communities, a procedural 'no' is heard very badly because there is usually a long and bitter, even if only half-remembered, history behind this relationship.

I was in a council flat doing a christening visit. All was going well. I thought it was slightly odd that the lad had kept his beanie on for the whole of the visit. Towards the end of the visit, I could tell he was working up to asking something. 'Vicar, do I have to take my hat off in church?' I answered without checking. 'Yes. It is a sign of respect for God that men take their hats off in church.' He took his beanie off. Half an ear was missing. 'I was attacked,' he told me. He was clearly deeply embarrassed and I could not repair the damage I had done. I was unthinkingly respectable and culturally and pastorally insensitive. I hope their baby was baptized somewhere else, because they never came back to me.

There are other groups now who also have long and bad memories of the Church saying a harsh 'no', particularly over sexual ethics. I think of the woman who had been put out of the Mothers' Union because she had divorced her abusive husband to protect herself and her children. Thirty years of alienation later, a supportive church member encouraged her to ask the vicar if he would remarry a divorcee. We did, and it was a service both of joy and reconciliation. I wonder if we realize how hostile as well as archaic the Church sounds with our endless internal and increasingly unreal debates about human sexuality.

The third test of authenticity is lack of snobbery. In other words, are vicars able to mix without condescension and treat different sorts of people with respect? Herbert knew this.

If there be any of the gentry or nobility of the parish, who sometimes make it a piece of state not to come at the beginning of the service with their poor neighbours, but at mid-prayers, both to their own loss and of theirs also who gaze upon them when they come in, and neglect the present service of God, he by no means suffers it, but after divers gentle admonitions, if they persevere, he causes them to be presented [taken to a church court].[6]

No privilege for the wealthy or socially 'superior'. The C of E has often found it hard to follow this example of moral courage. Herbert was – surprisingly? – sensitive to the sensitivities of social class. When he writes of 'the Parson's Courtesy', he describes the ideal of the vicar entertaining his parishioners. He invites everyone, because he is aware that people may interpret non-invitation as a slight. And he delights to entertain the poor at his own table, carving for them, 'who are much cheered by such friendliness'. But he also knows that sometimes it is more practically generous to give the poor money, 'which they can employ to their own advantage and suitably to their needs'.[7]

On the whole, people still do not swear in the presence of vicars. A young mum had found faith. She and her husband were members of the local motor-biking club. They invited me to go to one of their club evenings in the local pub. I had gone with a collar on but, without thinking, was also wearing a jumper with a high neck. I arrived a bit late, after the business part of the meeting had started. It was just like a PCC – 'I organized this on my own and no one f . . . ing helped me!' said the chair. And then, as the meeting ended, he said to my friends, 'I thought your mate, the f . . . ing vicar, was coming?' I shyly introduced myself. It is a moment of mischief

I remember with a smile to this day. We also used to run all-age nativity plays. The husband, who was not a regular church-goer, asked if he could take part. 'Yes, of course. Who do you want to be?' 'An angel,' he said. 'I've always wanted to be an angel!' And so an angel he was, complete with surplice and tinsel, swaying gently at the back of the heavenly host because he had had some worldly spirit to encourage him.

Sticky carpets and sofas or white fluffy rugs that we dare not stand on, chipped mugs or antique coffee cups – vicars take them all in their stride because we are Christ's ambassadors and Christ is there before us and with us, loving everyone. Our people know, somehow, that Jesus was not a snob.

The fourth test is simplicity. I hear regularly in schools about pollution and climate change. Our children and young people care about the planet they are inheriting. I have never felt scrutinized for my personal lifestyle. That is a relief, be-cause I am no moral exemplar here. If global warming is the biggest threat to humankind, then why is this not higher up my personal list of moral and spiritual priorities? Do I drive low-polluting cars, or does the diocese try to make vicarages energy efficient? Do I eat carefully and recycle thoroughly? Is the Church taking a lead in this area, or playing catch-up? What would be the power of my witness to my faith in God in Christ's creation if I lived more simply?[8] As a young Christian man, I was taught that my most important witness was not to swear and not to laugh at jokes about sex. Even then, how could I have got my priorities so wrong?[9] Simplicity of living is a much more powerful and faith-filled witness. Our people know, somehow, that Jesus was not rich and lived simply.

To put this in a nutshell: the Church is fallen and has much in its history that is sinful,[10] and repentance will require the

Church to live humbly now, to live down its abuse of power and wealth, to live down clerical abuse, to live down clerical autocracy. I think this is the most important element of the 'end of Christendom' but not often named[11] – though the Spirit appears to be trying to teach us some hard lessons now and is raising up leaders who model simplicity for us. Humility really is the key virtue for the Church in this age.

'Theology of the cardigan'

In most of the (working-class) parishes where I have served, only two sorts of people wore suits: head teachers and funeral directors. I respect their uniform but I had to decide on my uniform. Was I to become a grey man in a grey suit, signalling that I was part of the professional class? Sometimes, yes. But most of the time I was in a cardigan. This may have contributed to a certain 'sad' (uncool) appearance but it also communicated a certain (slightly odd perhaps) social standing. This was not power dressing. Almost always when on public duty the cardigan was graced by a dog collar. That is my uniform as a public representative of Christ and the Church. But dressed down and nuanced. How do vicars communicate their social status? Herbert again was here before us: 'The parson's . . . apparel [is] plain, but reverend and clean, without spots, or dust, or smell; the purity of his mind breaking out and dilating itself even to his body clothes, and habitation.'[12] I would not claim that wearing a cardigan is a sign of moral and spiritual purity, but outward signs can communicate deep messages about values.

How do we communicate that we are simple, like Jesus?

15

Jesus-likeness

I am male, fairly tall, with a (greying) beard, big nose and deep-set eyes. I know that in certain circumstances I can press some unconscious buttons in people about Jesus.

A young man had drowned in the Tyne. We did not know how he got in the water. Drink? Drugs? He was on a charge for 'TWOC' ('taking without the owners' consent'), was facing time in prison and was frightened. Did he jump? We will not know on earth. His funeral was packed, full of weeping young people. The wake was back at the family home, sitting out on the lawn, drinking whisky and tea. Talking. Listening. Grieving.

We used to get bother around the church – graffiti, vandalism, rubbish, low-level anti-social behaviour. I used to have to nerve myself to go out and talk to the young people, especially if I had seen them doing something wrong. After this lad's funeral everything was sweetness and light. 'He's all right. He did N's funeral. He's okay.' And they would chat and drift away happily. No more damage. It was slightly surreal. Who was I for them?

In this chapter we will explore the core of the calling to be a Christian, and thus to be a vicar, a public representative Christian. It is to be a disciple of Jesus and to strive to be like him.

This seemingly obvious statement is not uncontentious. First, simple imitation is simplistic. I am not, and nor are modern Christians, residents of the first century in Galilee and Judea. It is worse than naive to imagine we should or even could directly imitate the life of a wandering Jewish rabbi in AD 30. Second, likeness does not mean exact copying. Women can be like Jesus at least as well as men. Third, Jesus of Nazareth as we meet him in the Gospels is not always easy to understand. Imitation could be confusing. Fourth, Jesus is both truly human and truly God. He is one of us and also utterly unlike us.

But, fifth, his example is hugely challenging; much easier to find reasons not to have to try. And we noted in the last chapter the authenticity tests our cultural context applies to us – simplicity of living, especially about money, compassionate welcoming, lack of snobbery, simplicity of living applied to the planet. I would argue that we can justify this 'ordinary theology' with disciplined biblical and theological study. The proper expectations on vicars to be 'like Jesus' should not be dismissed.

Modelling the Incarnation

The corollary of the 'incarnational principle' surely is that vicars model themselves on the Incarnate One. This has not always been the case. I am struck by the ambivalence in Herbert. There is so much kindness and humility in *A Country Parson*, and yet again and again the vicar as an agent of moral and social control is the operative as well as the normative theology.[1] 'The Country Parson is in God's stead to his parish, and dischargeth God what he can of his promises. Wherefore there is nothing done either well or ill, whereof he is not the rewarder or punisher.'[2] Many vicars have not modelled themselves on a Christ recognizable to us from the Gospels. I am thinking not so much of the evidently corrupt,[3] rather about those who saw themselves as men responsible for enforcing God-given moral and social order.[4] So perhaps there is a deeper question here: what is our understanding and imagining of the Incarnate One?

We have already noted the paradigmatic text in Luke 4 where Jesus provides a summary of his mission. We have seen how this implies active engagement with the physical, psychological, emotional and spiritual needs of other people so that they can enter into the life-giving world of God's kingdom. We can now note how this was worked out in Jesus' ministry: through miraculous healings and deliverance, as well as the simplest of actions of touch and conversation; through preaching faith in a merciful heavenly Father, as well as enacting this mercy by gathering those who were not normally included; through teaching radically loving values, and then forgiving the ones who hurt him; through challenging powerful hypocrisy and corruption in word and action. And while embodying the depth of Jesus' cosmic meaning does lie beyond us, we share even in his journey of death, to defeat the power of sin and death, and resurrection to new life. That Luke is written the way it is demonstrates for us how Luke himself imagined the importance of imitating Jesus for himself and his Church.

We can amplify this from another source. We have spent much time with Hooker the ecclesiastical polemicist. We should now spend some time with Hooker the mystical theologian. Immediately following his fierce defence of the administration of the sacraments according to the Book of Common Prayer, Hooker embarks on a soaring consideration of the meaning of the Incarnation. It has an extraordinary tone to it.

And as Christ took manhood that by it he might be capable of death whereunto he humbled himself, so because *manhood* is the proper *subject* of *compassion* and *feeling pity*, which maketh the sceptre of Christ's regency even in the kingdom of heaven *amiable*, he which without our nature could not on earth suffer for the sins of the world, doth now also by means thereof both make intercession to God for sinners and exercise dominion over all men with a true, a natural, and a *sensible touch of mercy*.[5]

Here Hooker is building on Hebrews. Because in his incarnation Christ took into himself human nature, he also took into himself both knowledge of the human condition and the capacity for compassionate pity that is part of the human condition. Hence he treats humankind with a mercy that can be felt. I am used to expounding the Incarnation in such a way as to cite Jesus as the window into the true character of the Godhead: compassionate and merciful. Hence Jesus behaves with such compassion. Here, Hooker amplifies, even tweaks, this by pointing out the contribution of human nature to divine compassion. It is extraordinary but in keeping with his deep sense of human dignity.

Hooker then indulges in a lengthy discussion of patristic Christology before arriving at another of his purple paragraphs, which we can use as a theological engine for our reflections on the imitation of Christ.

Finally, sith [since] God hath deified our nature, though not by turning it into himself, yet by making it his own *inseparable habitation*, we cannot now conceive how God should without man either exercise divine power, or receive the glory of divine praise. For man is in both an associate of deity.[6]

I sometimes wonder if Hooker says more than he intended to say. The dignity that God in Christ has conferred on human-kind through the Incarnation is to make it his 'inseparable habitation'. God has joined God-self to humankind eternally, such that all God's working now, and even the praise of God, is possible because of and includes human nature. I am sure it is right to describe Hooker as 'the theologian of human dignity'.[7]

Therefore, if we take Luke and Hooker as our guides, we will imitate Jesus most when we establish and enhance human dignity.

It was chucking it down. We were about to lock up the church after a long morning. A bedraggled young woman arrived at the church door. She had no coat and on her feet she was wearing a pair of slippers with newspaper shoved in the holes. She was shivering with the cold. As we (three of us – safeguarding) sat in the vicarage chatting, the story came out: just out of prison, having spent her prison discharge grant, she was on her own in a hostel; her probation worker was off duty and she had no food left. We had a policy of not giving any money, but we did keep food in the church and vicarage, and in this case we also sourced a coat, a pair of shoes, some clothes, including some clean underwear. But the thing that made me cry was when she was going through our food box and found a can of hot dogs and shouted out in delight.

'For I was hungry and you gave me food, I was thirsty and you gave me something to drink, I was a stranger and you welcomed me, I was naked and you gave me clothing, I was sick and you took care of me, I was in prison and you visited me.' Then the righteous will answer him, 'Lord, when was it that we saw you hungry and gave you food, or thirsty and gave you something to drink? And when was it that we saw you a stranger and welcomed you, or naked and gave you clothing? And when was it that we saw you sick or in prison and visited you?' And the king will answer them, 'Truly I tell you, just as you did it to one of the least of these who are members of my family, you did it to me.' (Matthew 25.35–40)

This passage from Matthew feels like the sort of imitating that all Christians should do (and its paradigmatic place in Matthew suggests this is a correct reading) and that vicars get to do because people come to their churches and vicarages. This is the Jesus-likeness that is required of us. Though, as I have pondered this, it struck me it might also be Jesus-like to ask why young women are imprisoned for short periods, released without adequate support and why the probation service has been so deconstructed in recent years.

Jesus-likeness in the Ordinal

We can put this very simply: vicars are required to imitate Jesus deeply. The Ordinals teach this. So, alongside the newer language, the deacon is still required to imitate Jesus Christ the servant: 'Christ is the pattern of their calling and their commission; as he washed the feet of his disciples, so they must wash the feet of others.'[8] The ministry of Jesus Christ that deacons share is the ministry of Christ the servant.[9] This is of course the foundational ministry for all the ordained, for all are 'fellow servants'.[10] The priest is pointed to a different aspect of Jesus Christ to imitate – Christ the Good Shepherd: 'They are to set the example of the Good Shepherd always before them as the pattern of their calling.'[11] And at the culmination of the declarations, the priests are reminded that they are to grow into the 'likeness' of Christ, 'so that God may sanctify the lives of all with whom you have to do'.[12] In other words, it is as the priests imitate Christ that God is most powerfully at work.

This is a weighty calling. I am not for a moment suggesting that *only* the ordained are called to Jesus-likeness. That way lies a clericalist, dependent and dormant Church. No, this is the calling for all Christians. But the ordained are called to live this publicly and for the purpose of being instrumental blessings for the Church and world. It is a high and particular calling and, if we undermine it by subverting it for some other reason, even a good one like the flourishing of the whole people of God, then we will be undermining not just the vicars but their God-given role and responsibility. Vicars are to be Jesus-like because in that, however imperfectly, they make Jesus Christ publicly present to his Church and world. They are fragments of incarnation.

'You cannot bear the weight of this calling'

As I write this I feel both my utter inadequacy for this calling and also its slightly banal reality. I once gave a lecture that included a section on the 'vicar as a practical atheist'. I suggested, for example, it does not require faith, let alone theological training, to organize repairs to a boiler. If I could recoup the hours I spent standing staring at non-functioning church boilers, I would be a younger man. And in some of our settings – for example a school governing body assessing pupil data – to talk too swiftly of God is silly. And, if I am honest, much vicaring is not spiritually dynamic. I believe that God does miracles. It is just that most weeks I did not see any biblical-style miracles and I do *not* think that was to do with lack of faith or expectation. Much of our work as vicars is properly routine. Conversely, some of the time, as we have already noted in this book, it is profoundly challenging to a sense of trust in God.

It was August and I was sitting at my desk. Life was quiet. I was planning some routine visiting and even some filing. The phone rings. It is a bride whose wedding I conducted just a few weeks ago. I was about to launch into a bright and cheery 'How was the honeymoon?' conversation, when I heard the tone of her voice. It turned out that her 14-year-old nephew had been knocked down and killed in a traffic accident. It felt as if my world had stopped, let alone hers or her sister's. I can picture the chapel now filled with teenagers as we listened to his favourite songs. Atheism is a strange temptation at moments like that. In practice, the camber is the opposite: to embody and articulate the hope that despite and within this tragedy there is the loving presence of God.

But there is, I think, deep and pervasive pressure to turn vicars into practical atheists.

Staying close to Jesus

In that lecture, I suggested a number of ways of counteracting this pressure. One was to allow ourselves to be renewed in our sense of the big-ness, the otherness, of God; to remind ourselves that we do live in a God-shaped universe; to allow us space not to feel that we have to answer every question in it. I also suggested that we allow ourselves to be renewed in our faith in the *missio Dei*, the constant work of the midwife Spirit in the world, bringing life to birth. This is especially important when we have been with someone and then have to trust the Spirit with the next step. Above all, the key is to allow ourselves to be renewed in our experience of the immanence of Jesus Christ with us.

I believe in the Daily Office. (Rather, I believe in the God who meets with us in the Daily Office!) But I amplify it, when I am disciplined, by a daily reading from a Gospel. Jesus in the Scriptures is sometimes baffling, sometimes distant, sometimes uncomfortably challenging and sometimes immediately present. It does not suit everyone and it needs to be done in a structured, supported and accountable way, but the way of Ignatian meditation, of imagining ourselves into a story from the Gospels, culminating in an encounter with Jesus Christ, is powerful in itself. It also breaks down the gap between then and now so that the Gospels become alive in a new, sustained way.[13]

Of course, for colleagues from the Catholic tradition, this already happens: daily Mass = daily reading of a Gospel. It also means daily experience of Jesus Christ through the Eucharist. It is Jesus Christ's humility and humanity in coming to us sacramentally that I find most moving. Hear Herbert again on the humble tenderness of Jesus Christ:

> Not in rich furniture, or fine array,
>   Nor in a wedge of gold,
>   Thou, who from me wast sold,
>   To me dost now thy self convey . . .
>
> But by the way of nourishment and
>   strength

Thou creep'st into my breast;
Making thy way my rest,
And thy small quantities my length . . .

Only thy grace, which with these
elements comes,
Knoweth the ready way,
And hath the privy key,
Op'ning the soul's most subtle rooms.[14]

Notice how Jesus Christ comes to us modestly and gently –
in form and manner – but in such a way as produces deep
spiritual and personal rest and renewal.

Jesus-likeness has to be worked at. It is hard to sustain this
work when all the other pressures of vicaring are bearing in
on us. That is why simple disciplines that help this work to
happen routinely are so valuable.[15] I wonder if a good Anglican
way is in our own specific context to find means to meet Jesus
Christ in word and sacrament and world, every day and certainly every few days? The Church is most often and most passionately renewed when it returns to its focus on God in Jesus.
We are primarily disciples of Jesus, living in and leading the
community of the disciples of Jesus. That is our unique selling
point. To do that, we need to be like Jesus.

CONCLUSION

16
Success?

I was sitting in a warm comfy state during the sermon in a college Eucharist. We had a kind visiting preacher, a senior church leader from Cumbria, and it was one of the sheep parables. He was good on sheep, as one might hope for a minister from the Lake District. Then he stopped, took off his glasses and leaned over the pulpit. 'The Church is a very anxious institution. That makes it very dangerous. Be careful of it!' He put his glasses on and went back to talking about Herdwicks. I sat slightly baffled and glanced around. Other people were also slightly unnerved. Had that really just happened? Did we just hear that warning? We had done; they were wise words and have stayed with me ever since.

In an anxious Church, what is the true measure of success? Wise friends have queried my use of this word, 'success'. Surely we ought to be asking about 'fruitfulness' or even that old chestnut, 'faithfulness'. They are right, of course. But vicars are 'hearing' this language of success. Are our churches growing? If not, are we failing? So, in a Church where this question is more prominent, what is an Anglican measure of success?

One of my former vicars once joked with me: 'You know why vicars build things? It is so that they leave something tangible behind them when they go.' Having been a vicar, I now get the point. The combination of planning and delivering many one-off events alongside much work with people, who come and go, left me wondering sometimes what I was achieving. It all seemed rather ephemeral. So of course I did some tangible building work. But I remember often asking myself that painful question: 'What have I done of lasting value this year?'

Numbers count

I wonder if there is a legacy of snobbery about numbers in the C of E. 'Of course we don't count numbers here. So crass. "Bums on seats." Rather, it is all about depth and influence.' I understand that numbers are a crude measure. I also understand that there are fields where numbers grow easily and fields where the soil is harder, especially when it comes to encouraging people to institutional involvement with the Church. The gap between the numbers game in the urban priority areas and in the suburbs has been real for at least 170 years.[1] It is just the case that it is easier to grow large congregations in university cities than in pit villages. The C of E has normally shown wisdom and grace in recognizing this, though the current financial pressures make us increasingly vulnerable to numerical success shaping clergy deployment. If we are after big numbers, will we send our clergy to Easington, for example?[2] Thank God we still are.

But numbers do count. There are some simple equations in church life. More committed Christians = more Christian action. While we might be suspicious of the quality of faith behind the churchgoing culture of the Victorian era, that level of resource enabled a colossal impact on Victorian Britain, mostly for good.[3] The frequent lament in many of our parish churches is: 'We could do so much more if only we had more people.' There is sometimes no shortage of vision but there is a chronic shortage of people. We urgently need 'more labourers for the harvest'. We need not be bashful about seeking new Christians.

We have already noted our bashfulness about introducing people to Jesus Christ and how that is so painfully at odds with our personal experience of receiving life through Jesus. We have also already noted Temple's assertion about the Church being for its non-members and the problematic nature of this when it is interpreted as constraining our hope that others too will come into the mutuality of this relationship with Jesus Christ. But above all, we live as disciples of Jesus and point to his loving God: we do not sell a message or invite people to join a club.

Sometimes the C of E and its vicars are their own worst enemy. I don't underestimate the challenges of being a vicar and nor should we underestimate people's wariness of the Church and religion, and therefore that evangelism can be stony ground. But there are easy wins. We had organized a workshop to reflect on Anglo-Catholic church growth in London.[4] It was an excellent and encouraging presentation, but the most exciting part was the reaction of our northern clergy: 'It's not rocket science. We can do this!' We can offer a warm appropriate welcome, accessible but not thin worship, good relevant parish groups, with a living faith at the heart of it all. Growth can result from seeing differently and then doing differently, even if only a little. I was lamenting to a youth worker about our lack of young people's work. He looked back at me and said: 'What have you been doing in school with your confirmation class? You have been enabling a group to bond and to go on a spiritual journey together. Build on that!' I had been so fixed on the process of preparing the young people for confirmation that I had not seen what was being achieved by way of building 'church'. So, in time, these young people were encouraged to help create a new-style church youth group. 'It's not rocket science.' And while it is not as automatic as a mathematical equation, I am convinced that good quality parish work that flows from a healthy local church life does produce numerical growth. This is still possible for our parish churches. Numbers are a part of success.

'Unless a grain of wheat . . .'

When it comes to evaluating success, I wonder if there are lessons to be learned from society around us. The ceaseless pursuit of happiness does not appear to be successful. It is like trying to catch a butterfly in our hands. Either it is elusive and flies away or we catch it and crush it, destroying its life and beauty. Vicars are working for an anxious institution, anxious about its survival. If we go after the survival of the institution, however cleverly we disguise it, people see through us. The Church urgently needs active members and money. But if that is the message that is heard, then it is deeply off-putting. Who wants to join a failing, needy, institution anxious for its self-preservation? As church and vicars, we have to be aiming at other goals: being the midwife for people discovering a lasting, life-giving relationship with God and being a participant in the growth of the kingdom of God in our communities. It was the attraction of being part of a great missionary adventure with God that drew me into Christian discipleship and ministry. The Church grows as it is caught up in the *missio Dei*. I am not saying that the Church only grows as it dies to itself – the visible Church is too valuable for that – but I am saying that the Church only grows as it does not focus on itself but focuses on joining in with God in God's world. And there *is* an open-handedness about that.

We have already noted the huge range of activities into which vicars and local churches are drawn. Many of these do not generate an immediate return, either in terms of members or money. While I was working as a vicar, someone calculated that it costs the C of E £35 to have a stipendiary vicar in a room for an hour. I have no idea if that figure is accurate. But I do know that if covering that cost was a criterion for success, then I failed most days. Theologically, the ministry of parish churches and their vicars is rooted in the abundant generosity of God: 'poured out, heaped up, over-flowing'. It is exemplified in the love of God in Christ on the cross, which gives everything. I know that I caused our PCC treasurers some sleepless nights, but when I said to our PCCs, 'We are making a financial loss on many of our christenings', no one said, 'Well, if they are uneconomic, we will stop doing them.' There was the open-handed generosity of God embodied in three northern Anglican churches.

And unless I am misinterpreting the activity of God, much vicaring was not systematic but was real and mysterious. This is not an argument for being disorganized and unsystematic; but every week, like many church members, I would have an encounter with someone, normally unplanned, which was a sacramental moment. I could not discern the long-term plan of God for this individual life, but I did know that in that moment I had a small part to play. Clear-eyed strategy was hugely valuable. Good decisions about where to invest our limited time were essential, and were part of the *missio Dei*. The *missio Dei* is strategic but also mysterious, like the seed growing in the field. Never more so than when we are dealing with individuals. I am reminded of the narrative pattern of the Gospels. Jesus had a strategic plan and he followed it to the cross, but he also blessed individual after individual during his mission.

But – there is often a 'but' – we have also discussed the perils of the language of 'service', the open-handed giving of love or time or resource, without any expectation of return. It is a word beloved of our parish churches. But what if we add 'mutuality' or 'relationship' to this word 'service'? Is that a deeper measure of success? In other words, we should be looking for a collaborative ethos and outcome.

John used to come regularly to our curate's house for a sandwich and two mugs of tea. 'None of that crumbly cheese mind, it gets stuck in my beard.' He had a large beard. Over the years we learned that John had a flat somewhere and that his major hobby was betting on the horses. Even on a good day, I worried whether making the tea and sandwiches was a good use of my time. And on a bad day . . . One day he turned up as usual. It happened to be the day before our son's birthday. Before he left he took out of his bag a large bar of chocolate and a birthday card. 'That's for your boy. I didn't want to come tomorrow because I would have been in the way. Happy Birthday to him.' The card was still in its wrapper. Unsigned. Of course. John was illiterate. This was a sign of real relationship. If we had stayed longer in that parish, what might have come of it?

Measures of success

As I reflect back on my time as a vicar and look ahead to the time when I have to leave my current parish, even given the mysteriousness of joining in with the *missio Dei*, what are my real (operative) measures of success? There will of course be countless individuals touched by the love of Christ. There will be communities and institutions whose life has been enriched by the exposure of and to the kingdom of God. There will be signs of liberation for 'life in all its fullness'. The reputation of Christ will have been enhanced and there will be a good 'smell' about the Church. And, ironically perhaps in light of my earlier caution about the self-preserving anxieties of the C of E, the local church will be stronger: bigger, more able to lead, sustain and grow itself, and within that there will be individuals who have come to faith, discovered their own gifting and call to Christian ministry and who are now leading the church. And when I go, I will be barely missed. It is a high standard of success to meet. But then I think that vicaring is a demanding vocation, which the Church needs to honour and nurture.

If the 'parable of the sower' is indeed the vicar's parable, then I am praying for seed that will grow up to a hundred-fold. That is *other* people being fruitful in and for Christ. That is the deepest measure of the success of vicaring.

Blessing

We have noted in passing that one of the responsibilities reserved to the priest-vicar is blessing. This can often feel a bit strange. After all, 'God bless you' is a commonplace in everyday life and is a sign-off for some dodgy comedians! How or why should 'blessing' be managed by the Church? Because 'blessing' is a serious action. It is the public declaration by someone who is speaking on behalf of God that God approves of what is being done, of the people, the thing; that God is working for the good of the action, person or object. We are slowly thinking our way into the meaning and significance of blessing.[5] As so often, Herbert was here before us: 'The Country Parson wonders that blessing the people is in so little use amongst his brethren, whereas he thinks it not only a grave and a revered thing, but a beneficial also.' He went on to explain why:

Now blessing differs from prayer, in assurance, because it is not performed by way of request, but of confidence and power, effectually applying God's favour to the blessed, by the interesting of that dignity wherewith God hath invested the priest, and engaging God's own power and institution for a blessing.[6]

Notice the Classic Anglican word 'effectually'. It means that it really happens. God effects it. There is then that archaic use of the word 'interesting', which I take to mean here 'involving', 'including'. So the blessing comes as God works *with* the vicar collaboratively to deliver good power to the recipient. That sounds like Richard Hooker.

Blessing may seem an archaic place to finish a book on vicaring, but it is not.[7] Part of the role of the vicar is to be a visible channel of God's blessing. This is often in the form of words, but as the vicar tries to imitate Jesus, to be a fragment of the Incarnation, then so is Christ enabled to be present to individuals, institutions and communities. It is a blessing to be an instrument of blessing to others. Vicars are truly blessed.

We finish with one of the prayers from the service for the ordination of priests, which we pray as a blessing for those who are priest-vicars:

> Through your Spirit, heavenly Father,
> give these your servants grace and
> power
> to proclaim the gospel of your salvation
> and minister the sacraments of the new
> covenant.

Success?

Renew them in holiness,
and give them wisdom and discipline
to work faithfully with those committed to
      their charge.

In union with their fellow servants in
      Christ,
may they reconcile what is divided,
heal what is wounded
and restore what is lost.

May they declare your blessings to your
      people;
may they proclaim Christ's victory over
      the powers of darkness,
and absolve in Christ's name those who
      turn to him in faith;
so shall a people made whole in Christ
offer spiritual sacrifices acceptable to
      you,
our God and Father,
to whom, with the Son and the Holy
      Spirit,
belong glory and honour, worship and
      praise, now and for ever.
Amen.[8]

Notes

Preface

1 As an ecumenical discipline, I will use 'Church' to describe either the universal Church or a local visible branch of the universal Church and 'C of E' to describe the Church of England.

2 O. Chadwick, *The Victorian Church*, vol. 1, 3rd edn (London: A & C Black, 1971), p. 47.

3 This is a direct quotation of a senior member of the Archbishops' Council at a public Renewal and Reform symposium in 2018.

4 I noted these vicars in my acknowledgements in *A Passionate Balance* (London: Darton, Longman & Todd, 2007), but as two have subsequently gone to be with our Lord, I honour them again: Ken Morgan, Ted Roberts, Michael Webb, Richard Bateman, David Glover. And I am deeply indebted to the many other colleagues and former students who have taught me so much about vicaring.

5 Technically a vicar is an incumbent of a parish where tithes formerly passed to another body (often a monastery). So the vicar exercised ministry 'vicariously'. This contrasted with 'rector', who held the rights to ministry and money himself. All are now largely the same.

6 See <www.churchofengland.org/renewal-reform/setting-gods-people-free.aspx>.

7 For a recent first-hand, theologically reflective account of life as a woman priest, see Emma Percy, *What Clergy Do* (London: SPCK, 2014).

8 Books that have made a significant impact on me personally
include: S. Croft, *Ministry in Three Dimensions*, 2nd edn
(London: Darton, Longman & Todd, 2008); R. Etchells, *Set
My People Free* (London: HarperCollins, 1995); R. Greenwood,
Transforming Priesthood (London: SPCK, 1994); J. Martin and
S. Coakley (eds), *For God's Sake* (Norwich: Canterbury Press,
2016); S. Pickard, *Theological Foundations for Collaborative
Ministry* (Farnham: Ashgate, 2009); J. Pritchard, *The Life
and Work of a Priest* (London: SPCK, 2007); M. Smith, *Steel
Angels* (London: SPCK, 2014); G. Tomlin, *The Widening Circle*
(London: SPCK, 2014); S. Wells, *A Nazareth Manifesto* (Oxford:
Wiley-Blackwell, 2015). The book that has most filled my
imagination and spirit remains M. Ramsey, *The Christian Priest
Today*, rev. edn (London: SPCK, 1987).

1 Introduction

1 See Rowan Williams' introduction to *Mission-shaped
Church* (London: Church House Publishing, 2004), p. vii.
See also <www.freshexpressions.org.uk/guide-me/going-
deep-1-the-mixed-economy/> and <http://rowanwilliams.
archbishopofcanterbury.org/articles.php/2044/making-the-
mixed-economy-work>.

2 See <www.kcl.ac.uk/business/research/projects/experiences-of-
ministry.aspx>. Unpaginated.

3 See <www.churchofengland.org/renewal-reform/setting-gods-
people-free.aspx>. 'A great opportunity lies before us. It is the
same opportunity that has presented itself to the Church in
every decade for the last 100 years. It is an opportunity that
arguably has not been fully grasped since the days of Wesley.
Will we determine to empower, liberate and disciple the 98% of
the Church of England who are not ordained and therefore set

them free for fruitful, faithful mission and ministry, influence, leadership and, most importantly, vibrant relationship with Jesus in all of life? And will we do so not only in church-based ministry on a Sunday but in work and school, in gym and shop, in field and factory, Monday to Saturday?'

4 So, for example, Hooker (interestingly, contrary to the Preface to the Ordinal in the Book of Common Prayer) was clear that the New Testament did *not* provide a blueprint for how the Church was to be organized: 'Ye think that he which will perfectly reform must bring the form of church-discipline unto the state which then it was at. A thing neither possible, not certain, nor absolutely convenient. Concerning the first, what was used in the Apostles' times, the Scripture fully declareth not; so that making their times the rule and canon of church-polity, ye make a rule, which being not possible to be fully known, is as impossible to be kept' (*Laws of Ecclesiastical Polity*, Preface, 4.4, p. 109). (For ease of access, quotations are taken from the Everyman edition of Books I–V, R. Hooker, *Of the Laws of Ecclesiastical Polity*, ed. C. Morris (London and New York: J. M. Dent and Sons, 1965; first published 1907), and are cited book, chapter, section and page.) The Book of Common Prayer unselfconsciously includes John 20 and 21, Acts 6 and 20, Ephesians 4 and 1 Timothy 3 among its readings for the ordination services. These do not neatly cohere as a blueprint for church order. See J. D. G. Dunn, *Unity and Diversity in the New Testament* (London: SCM Press, 1977), ch. 6. This wisdom was forgotten as people adopted others' blueprints unreflectively. See even D. Watson, *I Believe in the Church* (London: Hodder & Stoughton, 1978). In an otherwise important book, Watson shows no awareness of what shaped this aspect of the C of E's history, and in his key chapters

(15 and 16) made no reference to the Anglican formularies.
Conversely, there is a commendation of lay eldership, which
had been specifically criticized by Hooker and which has,
strikingly, now almost disappeared from the C of E again
(see pp. 271ff.).

5 In *The Deployment and Payment of the Clergy* (London: Church
Information Office, 1964), Leslie Paul showed that the C of E
wouldn't be able to keep paying for its parochial clergy and
deploying them as it had done, and called for radical change.
In *A Strategy for the Church's Ministry* (London: Church
Information Office, 1983), John Tiller re-emphasized this and
argued for a radical reshaping of patterns of ministry with local
clergy (normally self-supporting and locally identified and
trained) and diocesan clergy who would be deployable to places
of complexity or crisis. Robin Greenwood has continued to
remind us of the urgency and nature of this task of moving to
a deeply collaborative model of priesthood. See *Parish Priests:
For the Sake of the Kingdom* (London: SPCK, 2009).

6 From Gregory VII, who in the twelfth century drove through a
deep renewal and reform of the Church by helping to improve
the discipline and quality of the clergy. I am indebted to
Michael Vasey for showing me this about myself.

7 I think this is the most cogent point made in the under-
evidenced A. Davison and A. Milbank, *For the Parish: A
Critique of Fresh Expressions* (London: SCM Press, 2013).

8 J. Martin and S. Coakley (eds), *For God's Sake* (Norwich:
Canterbury Press, 2016), pp. xv–xiv. Italics original.

9 This is potentially a contentious phrase. Some historical
theologians argue that we ought to restrict the word 'Anglican'
to the 1662 Settlement and afterwards, because it is only in
1662 that certain characteristics of Anglicanism were codified,

for example the absolute requirement for episcopal ordination. And we should note, of course, that the word 'Anglican' meaning a particular way of being Christian, as opposed to simply the English translation of the Latin word *anglicana*, meaning English, has its modern origins in the work especially of Cardinal Newman in his Anglican phase, when he meant by it a distinctive way of being a Catholic Christian, alongside the Roman and the Orthodox. I argue, conversely, that there is a common core to the first century of Reformation Anglicanism, traceable through Cranmer, Jewel and Hooker and exemplified in Herbert, and that when we are using historical material as a sounding board for current Anglican decisions, this period of 'Classic Anglicanism' is of particular weight.

10 See J. Lewis-Anthony, *If You See George Herbert on the Road, Kill Him* (London: Mowbray, 2009).

11 I would especially commend for parish clergy P. Ballard and J. Pritchard, *Practical Theology in Action: Christian Thinking in the Service of Church and Society*, 2nd edn (London: SPCK, 2006); L. Green, *Let's Do Theology* (London: Continuum, 2001); R. Osmer, *Practical Theology: An Introduction* (Grand Rapids, MI: Eerdmans, 2008).

12 A. Dulles, *Models of the Church*, expanded edn (New York: Doubleday, 2002).

13 O. Chadwick, *The Mind of the Oxford Movement* (Cambridge: Cambridge University Press, 1990), p. 62. No source given.

2 Whose world is it anyway?

1 *Common Worship: Ordination Services*, Study Edition (London: Church House Publishing, 2007), p. 37.

2 See the discussion in C. K. Barrett, *The Gospel According to John*, 2nd edn (London: SPCK, 1978), pp. 161–2.

3 Cyprian, Epistle 72, s. 21, in A. Roberts and J. Donaldson (eds) with A. Cleveland Coxe, *Ante-Nicene Fathers, Vol. 5 Hippolytus, Cyprian, Caius, Novatian* (1886, reprinted Peabody, MA: Hendrickson, 1995), p. 384.

4 The Westminster Confession, section 6, article 2, in G. Bray (ed.), *Documents of the English Reformation* (Cambridge: James Clarke, 1994), p. 492. Italics mine.

5 *The First Prayer Book of Edward VI*, first published 1549, in *The First and Second Prayer Books of Edward VI*, Everyman edn (London: J. M. Dent & Sons, 1910), p. 308.

6 For a longer critique of this theological perspective, see A. Bartlett, *Humane Christianity* (London: Darton, Longman & Todd, 2004), especially pp. 9–11.

7 *Ordination Services*, p. 37.

8 Bartlett, *Humane Christianity*, ch. 6.

9 This is part of a highly complex debate within Hooker scholarship. The majority view is that Hooker was self-consciously building on the Thomist inheritance. See F. Kerr, *After Aquinas* (Oxford: Blackwell, 2002), p. 97.

10 R. Hooker, *Of the Laws of Ecclesiastical Polity*, ed. C. Morris (London and New York: J. M. Dent and Sons, 1965; first published 1907), I.2.6, p. 154.

11 Hooker, *Laws* I.3.1, p. 154.

12 A recent author has argued that Hooker believed that the work of the Spirit was able to be seen most clearly through the functioning of human reason. N. Voak, *Richard Hooker and Reformed Theology* (Oxford: Oxford University Press, 2003), especially ch. 3. I think that Hooker's doctrine of the revelation of 'Divine Law' in Scripture trumps this but Voak's point reminds us of the weight Hooker gave to the interrelation of divine and human knowing.

13 W. David Neelands, 'Hooker on Scripture, Reason and "Tradition"', in A. S. McGrade (ed.), *Richard Hooker and the Construction of Christian Community: Medieval and Renaissance Texts and Studies* (Tempe, AZ: MRTS, 1997), p. 80.

14 From Hooker's 'Response' to 'Puritan' critiques of *Laws*. Cited by J. Booty, 'Hooker and Anglicanism', in W. Speed Hill (ed.), *Studies in Richard Hooker* (London: Cleveland Press of Case Western Reserve University, 1972), p. 218.

15 A. Bartlett, *A Passionate Balance* (London: Darton, Longman & Todd, 2007), pp. 44–51.

16 <www.churchofengland.org/prayer-and-worship/worship-texts-and-resources/common-worship/ministry/declaration-assent>. Italics mine.

17 B. Quash, *Found Theology* (London and New York: Bloomsbury T. & T. Clark, 2013), p. xiv.

18 Quash, *Found Theology*, p. xiv.

19 Subsequently reprinted with all further editions of the Book of Common Prayer.

20 'As for the act of excommunication, it neither shutteth out from the mystical [invisible], nor clean from the visible, but only from fellowship with the visible in holy duties.' Hooker, *Laws* III.1.13, p. 295.

21 Bartlett, *Passionate Balance*, pp. 121–32.

22 See <http://jimpunton.org.uk/life.htm>.

23 'Youth Work and Community – An Urban Ghetto – New York', <http://jimpunton.org.uk/life.htm>.

24 Bartlett, *Humane Christianity*, p. 126.

25 Bartlett, *Humane Christianity*, p. 149.

26 Stephen B. Bevans and Roger P. Schroeder, *Constants in Context: A Theology of Mission for Today* (Maryknoll, NY: Orbis Books, 2009), p. 7.

27 David J. Bosch, *Transforming Mission* (Maryknoll, NY: Orbis Books, 1996).

28 The reference is to Ezekiel 3.17; 33.7. *Ordination Services*, p. 37.

3 What on earth is the Church for?

1 I take this to be the implication of Cranmer's emphasis on reforming daily prayer in the Church and hoping that everyone would attend. See the closing paragraphs to Cranmer's essay, 'Concerning the Service of the Church', Book of Common Prayer, p. x.

2 A. Dulles, *Models of the Church*, expanded edn (New York: Doubleday, 2002), ch. 2. Interestingly, Dulles himself is most critical of this model.

3 Cf. N. Healy, *Church, World and the Christian Life* (Cambridge: Cambridge University Press, 2000). See his sophisticated discussion of the vocation of ecclesiology in ch. 2 and critique of 'blueprint ecclesiologies'.

4 See the surprisingly interesting A. Burns, *The Diocesan Revival in the Church of England* (Oxford: Oxford University Press, 1999).

5 These generalizations, which cannot be justified fully in a book of this length, are drawn in part from my own doctoral research on local church life in the nineteenth and twentieth centuries but have also been informed by the research of one of my doctoral students, on the life and possible futures of the C of E in North Yorkshire. See P. Bowes, 'Future Church: Envisioning the Church of England in Southern Ryedale in the Second Decade of the 21st century', DThM thesis, Durham University, 2012. The doctorate explores the unravelling of 'default Central Anglicanism' in this rural area, the loss of the widespread, if low-temperature, support on which local Anglican church life

had relied, and argues for the renewal of an 'intentional Central' theology and spirituality as realistic vehicle for renewal.

6 Dulles, *Models of the Church*, p. 198.

7 See A. Bartlett, 'Cranmer, Hooker and the Via Media', paper presented at the 'Invention of Anglicanism' Conference, Nottingham, 2003.

8 *The First Prayer Book of Edward VI*, first published 1549, in *The First and Second Prayer Books of Edward VI*, Everyman edn (London: J. M. Dent & Sons, 1910), p. 292.

9 A. Bartlett, 'Cranmer, Hooker and Ordination', paper presented to the Ecclesiastical History Society, 2002: 'In 1550 Cranmer included and in 1552 retained – as was traditional – the gospel reading from John 20 in the ordination of priests' service. It concluded with the powerful words: "Receive ye the Holy Ghost: whosesoever's sins ye remit, they are remitted unto them: and whosesoever's sins ye retain, they are retained." The very words then used by the Bishop in the formula as hands were laid on the new priests at ordination. Words that Cranmer translated from the Latin of the Pontificals and inserted here instead of Bucer's rather blander prayer . . . the effect was conservative and was to retain a focus on the role of the ordained in salvation.'

10 See G. Bray (ed.), *Tudor Church Reform: The Henrician Canons of 1535 and the Reformatio Legum Ecclesiasticarum* (Woodbridge: Boydell and Brewer, 2000).

11 R. Hooker, *Of the Laws of Ecclesiastical Polity*, ed. C. Morris (London and New York: J. M. Dent and Sons, 1965; first published 1907), V.77.1, p. 417.

12 Hooker, *Laws* V.77.1, p. 417.

13 Hooker, *Laws* V.77.8, p. 423.

14 Hooker, *Laws* V.77.2, p. 418.

15 Hooker, *Laws* V.77.3, p. 418.

16 Canon C1.2: 'No person who has been admitted to the order of bishop, priest, or deacon can ever be divested of the character of his order, but a minister may either by legal process voluntarily relinquish the exercise of his orders and use himself as a layman, or may by legal and canonical process be deprived of the exercise of his orders or deposed therefrom.' *The Canons of the Church of England*, 7th edn (London: Church House Publishing, 2017).

17 House of Bishops, *Eucharistic Presidency* (London: Church House Publishing, 1997), 6.3.

18 House of Bishops, *Eucharistic Presidency* 3.18.

19 House of Bishops, *Eucharistic Presidency* 4.45.

20 House of Bishops, *Eucharistic Presidency* 4.51.

21 Advisory Council for the Church's Ministry, *Education for the Church's Ministry*, Paper 22 (London: ACCM, 1987), paras 29 and 30.

22 Book of Common Prayer, 'The Ordering of Priests'.

23 Book of Common Prayer, 'The Making of Deacons'.

24 Hooker, *Laws* V.77.8, p. 423.

25 Hooker, *Laws* V.78.6ff., pp. 437ff.

26 Hooker, *Laws* V.78.5, p. 433.

4 The mysteries of place

1 We must not exaggerate this impression. In Bermondsey in the later nineteenth century as many incumbents left within five years as stayed for 21 years or more. A. Bartlett, 'The Churches in Bermondsey 1880–1939', PhD, University of Birmingham, 1987, p. 120.

2 See, for example, R. Lee, *The Church of England and the Durham Coalfields, 1810–1926* (Woodbridge: Boydell, 2007).

3 Cf. A. Rumsey, *Parish: An Anglican Theology of Place* (London: SCM Press, 2017), p. 112.

4 I am indebted to Will Foulger for informing my thinking in this area. See W. Foulger, 'Present in Every Place: The Church of England and the Parish Principle', DThM thesis, Durham University, 2018.

5 P. Sheldrake, *Spaces for the Sacred* (London: SCM Press, 2001), ch. 1.

6 P. Ward, *Liquid Church* (Eugene, OR: Wipf & Stock, 2013).

7 As one example, Z. Bauman, *Liquid Modernity* (Cambridge: Polity Press, 2000).

8 D. Goodhart, *The Road to Somewhere: The Populist Revolt and the Future of Politics* (London: C. Hurst & Co., 2017), pp. 25 and 4. Conversely, in London in 1851 over half of the over-20-year-olds had *not* been born in London. O. Chadwick, *The Victorian Church*, vol. 1, 3rd edn (London: A & C Black, 1971), p. 325.

9 Appropriately for the most technological generation, I turned to Wikipedia, which describes Gen Z as 'independent' with an 'entrepreneurial desire', after seeing their parents and older siblings struggle in the workforce. They are worried about debt and the shrinking opportunities for the middle class. The 'Great Recession' is a key formative experience along with 9/11. This leads to a 'feeling of unsettlement and insecurity among the people'. They are more risk averse and in the USA more likely to be churchgoers as young adults.

10 E. R. Wickham, *Church and People in an Industrial City* (London: Lutterworth Press, 1957).

11 Rumsey, *Parish*, p. 68.

12 Rumsey, *Parish*, p. 185.

13 While alert readers will have noted that I am implicitly critical of some of the argument in Davison and Milbank, *For the*

Parish, I commend its passionate valuing of good human community. A. Davison and A. Milbank, *For the Parish: A Critique of Fresh Expressions* (London: SCM Press, 2013).

14 A. Null, *Thomas Cranmer's Doctrine of Repentance: Renewing the Power to Love* (Oxford: Oxford University Press, 2001).

15 See Article 17. Also O. O'Donovan, *On the Thirty Nine Articles* (Exeter: Paternoster, 1986), pp. 82–7.

16 This is the wording from 1552. These words were unchanged in 1662.

17 See J. Inge, *A Christian Theology of Place* (Aldershot: Ashgate, 2003), ch. 5.

18 Rumsey, *Parish*, p. 186. Italics mine.

19 Commission on Urban Life and Faith, *Faithful Cities* (London: Church House Publishing, 2006), pp. 2ff.

20 G. Herbert, *A Country Parson* (first published 1652), ch. 35. I have used the Everyman edition, G. Herbert, *The Complete English Works* (London: David Campbell, 1995).

5 Signs of the kingdom

1 Pope Paul VI, *The Pastoral Constitution of the Church in the Modern World: Gaudium et Spes* (1965): '4. To carry out such a task, the Church has always had the duty of scrutinizing *the signs of the times* and of interpreting them in the light of the Gospel. Thus, in language intelligible to each generation, she can respond to the perennial questions which men ask about this present life and the life to come, and about the relationship of the one to the other. We must therefore recognize and understand the world in which we live, its explanations, its longings, and its often dramatic characteristics.'

2 <www.anglicancommunion.org/mission/marks-of-mission. aspx>.

3 Cf. S. Wells, *A Nazareth Manifesto* (Oxford: Wiley-Blackwell, 2015).

4 W. Temple, *Christianity and Social Order* (London: Penguin, 1942), ch. 7 and the famous Appendix. See also M. Brown (ed.), *Anglican Social Theology* (London: Church House Publishing, 2014).

5 G. Herbert, *A Country Parson*, ch. 12, in *The Complete English Works* (London: David Campbell, 1995).

6 Herbert, *Country Parson*, ch. 23, 'The Parson's Completeness'.

7 Irenaeus, *Against Heresies*, Bk 2, ch. X, section 3, in *Ante-Nicene Fathers* (Peabody, MA: Hendrickson, 1995), vol. 1, xxxviii.3, p. 522.

8 See David Ford, *Christian Wisdom* (Cambridge: Cambridge University Press, 2007), p. 46. I am choosing a different text from Ford's to treat as an imperative because I think this text enables the Church to speak into and live in a culture that is wrestling with human flourishing. See A. Bartlett, *Humane Christianity* (London: Darton, Longman & Todd, 2004), for a longer justification for this view.

9 W. Temple, *Readings in St John's Gospel* (London: Macmillan, 1955), p. 165.

10 Marianne Meye Thompson, *John: A Commentary* (Louisville, KY: Westminster John Knox Press, 2015), pp. 223–4. Italics mine. I am indebted to my colleague Richard Briggs for this reference.

11 Temple, *Christianity and Social Order*, p. 90. Italics mine.

12 The contrast with the first half of the twentieth century is striking, when the churches – mostly positively – encouraged the State (local and national) to take on many of these responsibilities because they were convinced that the State could do it more systematically, and therefore effectively and

fairly. See J. Cox, *English Churches in a Secular Society* (Oxford: Oxford University Press, 1982) for one of the clearest accounts of this process. I found the same in Bermondsey.

6 *In persona Christi* – and not

1 The vicar is also the 'Parson' or 'person' who embodies the presence of the Church, the body of Christ. Andrew Rumsey provides the legal reference from Blackstone's *Commentaries on the Laws of England* (1765): 'He is called parson, *persona*, because by her person the church, which is an invisible body, is represented; and he is in himself a body corporate.' A. Rumsey, *Parish: An Anglican Theology of Place* (London: SCM Press, 2017), p. 73.

2 The theology of *in persona Christi capitis* is much more developed in the Roman Catholic Church. See *The Catechism of the Catholic Church*, Part Two, 'The Celebration of the Christian Mystery', section 2, 'The Seven Sacraments of the Church', ch. 3, 'The Sacraments of Communion', Article 6, 'The Sacrament of Holy Orders', clause 1548: 'In the ecclesial service of the ordained minister, it is Christ himself who is present to his Church as Head of his Body, Shepherd of his flock, high priest of the redemptive sacrifice, Teacher of Truth. This is what the Church means by saying that the priest, by virtue of the sacrament of Holy Orders, acts in persona Christi Capitis', <www.vatican.va/archive/ccc_css/archive/catechism/p2s2c3a6.htm>. This theology can be traced back at least as far as John Chrysostom.

3 Though he also, scandalously, argued that given that episcopacy was indeed the work of the Spirit but subsequent to the giving of the law of God in the Scriptures, it was a pattern of church order that could be changed if the episcopate ever became an

obstacle to reform. R. Hooker, *Of the Laws of Ecclesiastical Polity*, ed. C. Morris (London and New York: J. M. Dent and Sons, 1965; first published 1907), VII.5.10.

4 House of Bishops, *Eucharistic Presidency* (London: Church House Publishing, 1997), para. 3.6.

5 Hooker, *Laws* V.78.2–4.

6 Faith and Order Advisory Group, *The Priesthood of the Ordained Ministry* (London: Church House Publishing, 1986), para. 109.

7 'The newly ordained priests were no longer specifically commissioned to offer sacrifice for the living and the dead' (*Priesthood of the Ordained Ministry*, para. 89).

8 Hooker, *Laws* V.77.2.

9 *Priesthood of the Ordained Ministry*, para. 142.

10 *Eucharistic Presidency*, para. 3.26.

11 Book of Common Prayer, the second Exhortation, printed within the Communion Service.

12 R. Brightman, *The English Rite*, Vol. 1 (London: Rivingtons, 1915), p. ccxix.

13 'All things considered and compared with that success which truth hath hitherto had by so bitter conflicts with errors in this point, shall I wish that men would give themselves to meditate with silence what we have by the sacrament and less to dispute of the manner how' (Hooker, *Laws* V.57.3).

14 See, for example, B. Palmer, *Reverend Rebels* (London: Darton, Longman & Todd, 1993), or G. Rowell, *A Vision Glorious* (Oxford: Oxford University Press, 1992). But it is best to read their original autobiographies and biographies. From a Roman Catholic perspective, see John Vianney, Padre Pio and Oscar Romero. Perhaps we ought to spend more time as priests holding these people before us, and the women who would have been wonderful priests if only they had been allowed.

15 G. Herbert, *A Country Parson*, ch. 22, in *The Complete English Works* (London: David Campbell, 1995).

16 From 'Love bade me welcome', also known as 'Love (III)', in Herbert, *The Complete English Works*, p. 184. See my extended discussion of this poem in A. Bartlett, *A Passionate Balance* (London: Darton, Longman & Todd, 2007), pp. 186ff.

17 G. Herbert, 'Aaron', in Herbert, *The Complete English Works*, p. 170.

18 Note Article 25: 'but rather they be *certain sure* witnesses, and *effectual* signs of grace'. Italics mine.

19 This is why, much needed as they are because the collective wisdom of the priesthood has been eroded and our context has changed, *Professional Guidelines for the Conduct of the Clergy*, rev. edn (London: Church House Publishing, 2015) are not a final substitute for spiritual and moral integrity. See also J. Harrison and R. Innes (eds), *Clergy in a Complex Age: Responses to the Guidelines for the Professional Conduct of the Clergy* (London: SPCK, 2016).

20 See the lengthy discussion on reconciliation in *Priesthood of the Ordained Ministry*, pp. 45ff., for an account of how varied views were on this in the medieval period, let alone the Reformation.

21 *Common Worship: Services and Prayers for the Church of England* (London: Church House Publishing, 2000), p. 180.

22 Article 26, 'Of the worthiness of ministers'. 'Although in the visible Church the evil be ever mingled with the good, and sometimes the evil have chief authority in the Ministration of the Word and Sacraments, yet forasmuch as they do not the same in their own name, but in Christ's, and do minister by his commission and authority, we may use their Ministry, both in hearing the Word of God, and in receiving of the Sacraments.

Neither is the effect of Christ's ordinance taken away by their wickedness, nor the grace of God's gifts diminished from such as by faith and rightly do receive the Sacraments ministered unto them; which be effectual, because of Christ's institution and promise, although they be ministered by evil men.'

23 *Priesthood of the Ordained Ministry*, para. 146.

7 No more FKB ('Father knows best')

1 See H. Venn, *The Native Pastorate and Organization of Native Churches* (first published 1851) in R. P. Flindall (ed.), *The Church of England 1815–1948* (London: SPCK, 1972), and C. Peter Williams, *The Ideal of the Self-governing Church* (New York: Brill, 1990).

2 R. Allen, *Missionary Methods: St Paul's or Ours?* (Eastford, CT: Martino Fine Books, 2011; first published 1912).

3 E. R. Robert, *Partners and Ministers* (London: Falcon, 1972), p. 11.

4 <www.churchofengland.org/sites/default/files/2017-11/GS%20 Misc%202056%20Setting%20God%27s%20People%20Free. pdf>, p. 2, and <www.churchofengland.org/SGPF>.

5 Faith and Order Advisory Group of the Church of England, *The Mission and Ministry of the Whole Church*, GS Misc. 854 (London: Archbishops' Council, 2007), p. 1. It is worth noting the next sentence: 'These changes have tended to take place in a piecemeal fashion, rather than as the result of any overall strategy, and the issue the Church of England is now faced with is how to make sense of the new patterns of ministry that have developed, both theologically and practically.'

6 For a superb theological underpinning to this, see S. Pickard, *Theological Foundations for Collaborative Ministry* (London: Routledge, 2009).

7 *Common Worship: Ordination Services*, Study Edition (London: Church House Publishing, 2007), p. 10. Italics mine.

8 This is too complex an argument for the main text, but one of the ironies of the Oxford Movement was that, while it was founded on the authority of the episcopate, it generated persistent disobedience to the actual bishops of the C of E. And as the attempt to compel obedience by legal means collapsed in the last quarter of the nineteenth century, so was reinforced the sense that vicars were entirely independent. See P. Nockles, *The Oxford Movement in Context: Anglican High Churchmanship 1760–1857*, rev. edn (Cambridge: Cambridge University Press, 2008), or B. Palmer, *Reverend Rebels* (London: Darton, Longman & Todd, 1993).

9 See <www.churchofengland.org/sites/default/files/2017-11/GS%202072%20Clergy%20Wellbeing.pdf>, para. 7. And see the groundbreaking Y. Warren, *The Cracked Pot: The State of Today's Anglican Parish Clergy* (Stowmarket: Kevin Mayhew, 2002).

10 Book of Common Prayer, from 'The Ordering of Priests'.

11 *Ordination Services*, p. 39.

12 *Ordination Services*, p. 32.

13 *Ordination Services*, p. 37.

14 J. F. Friendship, *Enfolded in Christ* (Norwich: Canterbury Press, 2018), p. 131.

15 Friendship, *Enfolded in Christ*, p. 123.

8 The Chief Exec?

1 <www.insights.com >. This is a personality test that helps people to identify their preferred leadership styles. It has proved illuminating for our clergy.

2 <www.myersbriggs.org>. This is the most popular personality type indicator and is based on Jungian typology.

3 APEST – Apostle, Prophet, Evangelist, Shepherd, Teacher – is a psychological profiling test, related to the list of ministries in Ephesians 4. See A. Hirsch, *The Forgotten Ways*, 2nd edn (Grand Rapids, MI: Brazos Press, 2016), and <www.theforgottenways. org/what-is-apest.aspx>. While I have reservations about some of the claims made for APEST, and from an Anglican perspective would want to have a conversation about the relationship between this text and the threefold order, nonetheless it is remarkably effective at helping clergy to own their personal gifting and to enable their teams to discover their particular callings. It is fascinating that this passage is set in the BCP ordination services for priests and referred to in the ordination prayer over both priests and bishops. For bishops, I am sure that the linkage is to the calling of an apostle. This is confirmed by the readings from Acts 20 and John 20. I am less clear why it is used in the service for the ordination or priests. I don't think it is because the priest is supposed to exercise all these ministries. I suspect that the priest's is the ministry of 'pastor'. 'Apostle' was the bishop. 'Prophet' was believed to have been discontinued – 'dispensationalism'. 'Doctor' was a technical term for theological scholars, and 'evangelist' had again a meaning as a role in the early Church, though I guess that Cranmer might have also thought of this role as including proclaiming the true faith in Tudor England. And of course the other Bible readings for the ordination of priests focus on the role of the priest as 'shepherd'.

4 Slowly, vicars are having to recognize that incumbents will now almost always have an *episcopal* role in terms of the oversight of several former parishes. The groundwork for this shift in thinking came originally in the Tiller Report but more substantially, specifically and effectively in S. Croft, *Ministry*

in Three Dimensions, 2nd edn (London: Darton, Longman & Todd, 2008).

5 See <www.kcl.ac.uk/business/research/projects/experiences-of-ministry.aspx>.

6 As part of Renewal and Reform, the C of E established a task group 'to consider constraints caused to the mission and growth of the Church of England by existing canons, legislation, regulations and procedures, and to bring forward options and proposals for simplification and deregulation.' See <www.churchofengland.org/simplification.>

7 For support, see the excellent United Kingdom Church Administrators Network, <www.churchadministrators.net/>, and also the work of John Truscott, founder of Administry, <www.john-truscott.co.uk/>.

8 G. Herbert, *A Country Parson*, ch. 1, in *The Complete English Works* (London: David Campbell, 1995).

9 Herbert, *Country Parson*, ch. 20.

10 Herbert, *Country Parson*, ch. 6.

11 <https://churchmissionsociety.org/partnership-missional-church>.

9 Joy and throne and hair shirt: the Bible and vicaring

1 G. Herbert, *A Country Parson*, ch. 7, in *The Complete English Works* (London: David Campbell, 1995).

2 See P. Avis, *In Search of Authority* (London: Bloomsbury, 2014), pp. 47–52, for a sophisticated discussion of English Reformation perspectives on the authority of Scripture. Cf. C. Buchanan, *Is the Church of England Biblical?* (London: Darton, Longman & Todd, 1998), ch. 1, for a full discussion of what is implied in the priority that the C of E gives to Scripture. For a more provocative (funny if perhaps not fully reliable) view

of Anglican theology of Scripture, see R. Giles, *How to Be an Anglican* (Norwich: Canterbury Press, 2003), ch. 5.

3 For an analysis of Cranmer's own hermeneutics as exemplified in the Homilies, see R. Briggs, 'The Christian Hermeneutics of Cranmer's Homilies', *Journal of Anglican Studies* 15:2 (2017), pp. 167–87.

4 R. Hooker, *Of the Laws of Ecclesiastical Polity*, ed. C. Morris (London and New York: J. M. Dent and Sons, 1965; first published 1907), V.22.1, pp. 80–1. He goes on to mock the Puritans for suggesting that Scripture was provided by God so that it could be preached, for it was by preaching that grace comes. As if the 'chiefest cause' of 'committing the sacred Word of God unto books, is surmised to have been, lest the preacher should want a text whereupon to scholy' (*Laws* V.22.7, p. 86).

5 Hooker, *Laws* V.22.4, p. 82.

6 Canon A5, *The Canons of the Church of England*, 7th edn (London: Church House Publishing, 2017).

7 R. Williams, *Anglican Identities* (London: Darton, Longman & Todd, 2004), p. 2. Italics mine.

8 The place of the Bible in Anglicanism is explored at greater depth in A. Bartlett, *A Passionate Balance* (London: Darton, Longman & Todd, 2007), ch. 3.

9 See R. Greer, *Anglican Approaches to Scripture* (New York: Herder & Herder, 2006).

10 Herbert, *Country Parson*, ch. 7.

11 Hooker, *Laws* III.11.6, p. 338.

12 Hooker, *Laws* I.14.4, p. 217.

13 T. Cranmer, 'A Fruitful Exhortation to the Reading and Knowledge of Holy Scripture', Homily One in *Sermons, or Homilies* (Lewes: Focus Christian Ministries Trust, 1986; first published 1547), p. 5.

14 There is an embarrassment of riches from J. Goldingay and Tom Wright in the 'For Everyone' series, to more detailed work in 'treating the Bible with full imaginative seriousness'. See R. W. L. Moberly, *Old Testament Theology: Reading the Hebrew Bible as Christian Scripture* (Grands Rapids, MI: Baker Academic, 2013). A classic of Anglican spirituality that still deserves more prominence as an example of Anglican biblical theology is W. Temple, *Readings in St John's Gospel* (London: Macmillan, 1945).

15 See, for example, M. Basil Pennington, *Lectio Divina: Renewing the Ancient Practice of Praying the Scriptures*, 2nd edn (New York: Crossroad, 1998).

16 See, for example, R. W. L. Moberly, 'Theological Interpretation, Second Naiveté, and the Rediscovery of the Old Testament', *Anglican Theological Review* 99:4 (2017), pp. 651–70, and R. Briggs, *Reading the Bible Wisely*, rev. edn (Eugene, OR: Cascade Books, 2011).

17 Other suggestions for keeping the Bible fresh, which have come from wise colleagues, include: read a whole Gospel at a sitting once a year; read passages out loud (as they were often designed to be encountered); ask open questions – 'What does this say to us?' – and don't be frightened to say in the pulpit, 'I don't know'; get a 'Scripture mentor' as well as a 'spiritual director'; read Jewish commentators on the Scriptures.

18 <www.godlyplay.uk/>.

19 See A. Bartlett, *Looking through Jesus* (Stowmarket: Kevin Mayhew, 2017) for an example of these sorts of study.

10 Sacraments of the present moment

1 See the carefully nuanced discussion in R. Hooker, *Of the Laws of Ecclesiastical Polity*, ed. C. Morris (London and New York:

J. M. Dent and Sons, 1965; first published 1907), V.58–61,
pp. 237–57.

2 For the methodology of 'ordinary theology', see J. Astley,
Ordinary Theology (Aldershot: Ashgate, 2002).

3 For high-quality recent research into the meaning mothers are
attaching to infant baptism, see A. Fenton, 'Meaning-Making
for Mothers in the North East of England: An Ethnography
of Baptism', DThM, Durham University, 2017, and H. Rait,
'Belonging without Attending? A Qualitative Investigation of
the Reasons Non-churchgoers in Shotton Colliery Bring their
Children for Baptism', MA, Durham University, 2018.

4 The Revd (soon to be Dr) Paulette Gower.

5 A. Bartlett, *A Passionate Balance* (London: Darton, Longman &
Todd, 2007), pp. 121ff.

6 R. T. France, '"Not One of Us": An Exposition of Mark 9.38–41',
in G. Kuhrt (ed.), *To Proclaim Afresh: Evangelical Agenda for the
Church* (London: SPCK, 1995). Hearing this teaching delivered
was one of the moments when I realized why I love being an
Anglican, but no one had ever explained to me why it is so good.

7 Bartlett, *A Passionate Balance*, p. 185.

8 See, for example, the 'Engel Scale', <https://en.wikipedia.org/
wiki/Engel_scale>.

9 See, from an earlier generation, W. Carr, *Brief Encounters*
(London: SPCK, 1985), pp. 41ff., for a theological justification
for the occasional offices: 'The world is God's', 'Christian life is
a dialect existence', 'Grace is not cheap', 'The priority of grace'.

10 The Archbishops' Council, *Common Worship: Pastoral Services*
(London: Church House Publishing, 2000), p. 136: 'The Bible
teaches us that . . .'.

11 Notice how Hooker subverts that argument in his brief *Laws*
V.75, pp. 401–7.

12 Jean-Pierre de Caussade, *The Sacrament of the Present Moment* (first published 1861).

13 This is where I disagree with Alan Billings, whose excellent *Secular Lives, Sacred Hearts* (London: SPCK, 2004) has done more than any other to help my curates to understand the anthropology of the occasional offices. But his ecclesiology and soteriology, that we are simply the servant Church offering a service, detached from the Church as the community of the disciples of Jesus (to which we rightly long for all to belong), is deficient.

14 See <https://churchsupporthub.org> and the hugely important S. Millar, *Life Events* (London: Church House Publishing, 2018).

15 I am indebted to my colleague Sophie Jelley for these questions.

16 Hooker, *Laws* V.62, pp. 257–79.

11 'You're the man who talks about God': evangelism neither bashful nor cheesy

1 See, as just one example, T. Yates (ed.), *Bryan Green Parson-Evangelist* (Thame: Bryan Green Society, 1984). From a different tradition, note Robert Dolling's comment in defence of both High Mass and gospel-hall-style services: 'saying Evensong every night, you would certainly have neither of the dangers, but, on the other hand, you would have none of the educational or heart-touching power.' So he wrote new Christian hymns to familiar tunes, like 'Home, Sweet Home'. See B. Palmer, *Reverend Rebels* (London: Darton, Longman & Todd, 1993), p. 176.

2 This is LYCiG's model of evangelism – Prayer, Presence, Proclamation, Persuasion. See LYCiG, *Leading Your Church into Growth* Course Handbook (2018), pp. 40–1. Cited with permission. Because of its focus on parish-church-based evangelism and growth, I think LYCiG is one of the most

valuable agencies helping vicars and their churches to flourish:
.

3 This quotation is always unreferenced. Consultation with
Temple scholars reveals that it does *not* feature in Temple's
published work but oral testimony from those who worked with
him confirms the accuracy of the quotation. I am grateful to
Stephen Spencer for this information.

4 For an honest and thoughtful wrestling with this issue, see
G. Wakefield, *Doing Evangelism Ethically*, Evangelism 108
(Cambridge: Grove Books, 2014).

5 John N. Collins, *Diakonia: Reinterpreting the Ancient Sources*
(Oxford: Oxford University Press, 1990), and the excellent
summary and reflection in R. Brown, *Being a Deacon Today*
(Norwich: Canterbury Press, 2005), pp. 13ff.

6 *Common Worship: Ordination Services*, Study Edition (London:
Church House Publishing, 2007), pp. 15, 37.

7 <www.messychurch.org.uk/>.

8 See clear evidence for this in G. Wakefield, *Conversion Today*,
Evangelism 75 (Cambridge: Grove Books, 2006).

9 In a territorial church with many occasional offices, the
parish priest as the public face of the Church is crucial. It
remains striking how many people find their way to Christ via
relationship with their vicar. See J. Finney, *Finding Faith Today*
(Swindon: Bible Society, 1996) for slightly dated evidence of the
key role of C of E parish clergy in growth in our denomination,
but it still resonates with my experience.

12 Self-fulfilment or self-sacrifice or self-fulfilment?

1 F. Bridger, 'A Theological Reflection', in *Guidelines for the
Professional Conduct of the Clergy*, rev. edn (London: Church
House Publishing, 2015).

2 See A. Haig, *The Victorian Clergy* (London: Croom Helm, 1984) for a historical account of the professionalization of the Victorian clergy, including the creation of the theological colleges and also the development of clergy handbooks. Or M. Percy, *Clergy: The Origin of the Species* (London: Continuum, 2006) for a more sociological approach.

3 General Synod, *A Covenant for Clergy Care and Wellbeing*, First Draft for Consultation (London: Church House Publishing, 2018).

4 *Daily Telegraph*, 12 December 2017, and *The Guardian*, 1 February 2018.

5 M. Clinton and T. Ling (eds), *Effective Ministerial Presence and What It Looks Like in Practice: Insights from the Experiences of Ministry Project 2011–17* (London: King's Business School, 2017), unpaginated.

6 General Synod, *A Covenant for Clergy*, section 20.

7 Clinton and Ling, *Effective Ministerial Presence*.

8 See the extraordinary essay by Rowan Williams that both bases the Christian faith in the resurrection and then stiffens the traditional Anglican handling of the Incarnation by rooting it in the cross and the judgement of Christ. R. Williams, 'Beginning with the Incarnation', in *On Christian Theology* (Oxford: Blackwell, 2000), pp. 79–92.

9 *Common Worship: Ordination Services*, Study Edition (London: Church House Publishing, 2007).

10 *Guidelines for the Professional Conduct of the Clergy*, section 2.9.

11 *Guidelines for the Professional Conduct of the Clergy*, section 2.3.

12 I have found the following to be helpful books in checking my self-discipline in this area: J. F. Friendship, *Enfolded in Christ*

(Norwich: Canterbury Press, 2018) and J. Allain-Chapman, *Resilient Pastors* (London: SPCK, 2012). See also section 14 of *Guidelines for the Professional Conduct of the Clergy.*

13 The most famous example is the 2014 Office of National Statistics job satisfaction survey where vicars were top! See J. Harrison and R. Innes (eds), *Clergy in a Complex Age: Responses to the Guidelines for the Professional Conduct of the Clergy* (London: SPCK, 2016), p. 100.

13 Are vicars sad?

1 G. Herbert, *A Country Parson*, ch. 27, in *The Complete English Works* (London: David Campbell, 1995).

2 Indeed, in ch. 11 he advocated entertaining his parishioners in his home regularly, including sitting the poor next to him and carving for them 'who are much cheered with such friendliness'.

3 See the discussion in A. Bartlett, *Humane Christianity* (London: Darton, Longman & Todd, 2004), p. 69.

4 A. Rumsey, *Parish: An Anglican Theology of Place* (London: SCM Press, 2017), p. 74.

5 See the discussion in A. Bartlett, *A Passionate Balance* (London: Darton, Longman & Todd, 2007), pp. 182ff., and, behind that, A. Null, *Thomas Cranmer's Doctrine of Repentance: Renewing the Power to Love* (Oxford: Oxford University Press, 2001).

6 Book of Common Prayer, from the Exhortation to those about to receive communion.

7 Book of Common Prayer, Absolution in Morning and Evening Prayer. We should note that there is a discussion about Cranmer's own predestinarian views. I suggest that while this may have been Cranmer's private opinion, his public liturgy embodies and exudes a welcome to all to be saved.

8 S. Wells, *Improvisation: The Drama of Christian Ethics* (Grand Rapids, MI: Brazos Press, 2004), pp. 127–42. I am grateful to Hannah Rait for this reference.

9 G. Herbert, 'The Call', in Herbert, *The Complete English Works*, p. 153.

10 Herbert wrote four poems with the title 'Affliction'. For further reading, see J. Drury, *Music at Midnight* (London: Penguin, 2004), W. Cope, *George Herbert: Verse and Prose* (London: SPCK, 2002), P. Sheldrake, *Love Took My Hand: The Spirituality of George Herbert* (London: Darton, Longman & Todd, 2000).

11 G. Herbert 'The Agony', in Herbert, *The Complete English Works*, p. 34.

12 This phrase comes of course from Gerard Manley Hopkins' extraordinary poem 'God's Grandeur': 'The world is charged with the grandeur of God./ It will flame out, like shining from shook foil.'

13 H. Nouwen, *Clowning in Rome* (London: Darton, Longman & Todd, 2001), p. 3.

14 J. Cotter, *Yes Minister* (Sheffield: Cairns Publications, 1992), p. 41, quoted only in part.

14 'Do justice . . . love kindness . . . walk humbly with your God'

1 See of course Anthony Trollope, *The Chronicles of Barsetshire* (1855–67); and, more ferociously, R. Tressell, *The Ragged-trousered Philanthropists* (1914).

2 G. A. Patrick, *The Miners' Bishop: Brooke Foss Westcott* (London: Epworth Press, 2004). Westcott was the first Bishop of Durham to intervene actively on behalf of the miners during one of the frequent bitter strikes. Westcott forced through the inauguration of a Miners' Service in Durham Cathedral

as part of Miners' Gala Day; speaking at it was one of his last engagements, which he forced himself to undertake, just before he died. He is still honoured to this day, as is Bishop David Jenkins. Jenkins' funeral was graced by the Durham Miners' Association Band and banners from the pit villages.

3 K. Marx, *The Communist Manifesto* (1848).

4 See M. Westphal, *Suspicion and Faith: The Religious Uses of Atheism* (New York: Fordham University Press, 1998). He recommends reading Marx, Freud and Nietzsche as a Lenten discipline.

5 G. Herbert, *A Country Parson*, ch. 3, in *The Complete English Works* (London: David Campbell, 1995).

6 Herbert, *A Country Parson*, ch. 3.

7 Herbert, *A Country Parson*, ch. 11.

8 C. Foster and D. Shreeve, *How Many Lightbulbs Does It Take to Change a Christian?* (London: Church House Publishing, 2007) and *Don't Stop at the Lights* (London: Church House Publishing, 2008). See also as alternative sources of resources: Operation Noah, <http://operationnoah.org/resources/>; Christian Ecology Link, <https://greenchristian.org.uk/>; A Rocha, <https://arocha.org.uk/>.

9 Not that I am advocating swearing. It is still restricted under the terms of *Guidelines for the Professional Conduct of the Clergy*: 'Blasphemous, violent or offensive language or behaviour is unacceptable at all times' (section 10.10).

10 A. Bartlett, *Humane Christianity* (London: Darton, Longman & Todd, 2004), ch. 1, explores the causes of 'inhumane Christianity'. For others who are naming and wrestling with our task of moving on from oppressive church, see D. Edwards, *The Church that Could Be* (London: SPCK, 2002); B. McLaren, *The Great Spiritual Migration: How the World's Largest Religion*

is *Seeking a Better Way to Be Christian* (London: Hodder & Stoughton, 2017); D. Tomlinson, *Black Sheep and Prodigals: An Antidote to Black and White Religion* (London: Hodder & Stoughton, 2018). From a previous generation, see E. Schillebeeckx, *The Church with a Human Face* (London: SCM Press, 1985).

11 A brave and poignant exception is Jim Cotter. See his 'It Shall Not Be So Among You: A Litany of Repentance for Misuse of Authority in the Church'.

12 Herbert, *Country Parson*, ch. 3.

15 Jesus-likeness

1 See H. Cameron, *Talking about God in Practice: Theological Action Research and Practical Theology* (London: SCM Press, 2010) for the helpful distinction between 'operative' theology (what we actually believe and live by), 'espoused' theology (what we say we believe), 'formal' theology (what our institution says we believe) and 'normative' theology (what we should believe).

2 G. Herbert, *A Country Parson*, ch. 20, in *The Complete English Works* (London: David Campbell, 1995).

3 F. Butler-Gallie, *Field Guide to the English Clergy* (London: OneWorld Publications, 2018).

4 See many examples in M. Hinton, *The Anglican Parochial Clergy* (London: SCM Press, 1994). Hinton writes to celebrate English Anglican parochial ministry, but we must not lose sight of the many references to the authority of the clergy that he describes.

5 R. Hooker, *Of the Laws of Ecclesiastical Polity*, ed. C. Morris (London and New York: J. M. Dent and Sons, 1965; first published 1907), V.51.3, p. 203. Italics mine.

6 Hooker, *Laws* V.54.6, p. 216. Italics mine.

7 A. Bartlett, *Humane Christianity* (London: Darton, Longman & Todd, 2004), p. 63.

8 *Common Worship: Ordination Services*, Study Edition (London: Church House Publishing, 2007), p. 10.

9 *Ordination Services*, p. 17.

10 *Ordination Services*, p. 22.

11 *Ordination Services*, p. 32.

12 *Ordination Services*, p. 37.

13 D. Lonsdale, *Eyes to See, Ears to Hear: Introduction to Ignatian Spirituality* (London: Darton, Longman & Todd, 2000), and the classic Gerard W. Hughes, *God of Surprises*, 3rd edn (London: Darton, Longman & Todd, 2008).

14 G. Herbert, 'The H. Communion', in Herbert, *The Complete English Works*, p. 49.

15 See A. Clitherow, *Into Your Hands* (London: SPCK, 2001) for a much deeper exploration of the disciplines and gifts of prayer for parish clergy; interestingly also based on reflection on a Gospel narrative.

16 Success?

1 I am referring to the differential in reported church attendance in the 1851 Religious Census in England, where Shoreditch was the area with the lowest percentage of church attendance: Archbishop of Canterbury's Commission on Urban Priority Areas, *Faith in the City* (London: Church House Publishing, 1985), section 2.6. A very complex historiographical debate surrounds the issue of working-class church attendance. For a brief survey, see H. McLeod, *Religion and the Working Class in Nineteenth-Century Britain* (London: Macmillan, 1984).

2 For many years after the closure of the mines, Easington District was the poorest in England. It is *Billy Elliot* territory.

3 See, for example, D. Bowen, *The Idea of the Victorian Church* (Montreal: McGill University Press, 1968).

4 T. Thorlby, *A Time to Sow: Anglican Catholic Church Growth in London* (London: Centre for Theology and Community, 2017).

5 A. Davison, *Blessing* (Norwich: Canterbury Press, 2016); R. Greenwood, *Sharing God's Blessing: How to Renew the Local Church* (London: SPCK, 2016); R. Parker, *Rediscovering the Ministry of Blessing* (London: SPCK, 2014).

6 G. Herbert, *A Country Parson*, ch. 36, in *The Complete English Works* (London: David Campbell, 1995).

7 See, notably, G. Tomlin, *The Widening Circle* (London: SPCK, 2014).

8 *Common Worship: Ordination Services*, Study Edition (London: Church House Publishing, 2007), p. 43.

About the author

Alan Bartlett has been an Anglican priest for 27 years. He has served in four north-eastern parishes as well as teaching in a theological college, where he was the postgraduate director, and is now working as a Continuing Ministerial Development (CMD) officer in Durham. Alan taught Anglicanism, church history, spirituality and practical theology. He has written widely on Anglicanism and spirituality and now reflects on the future of English Anglican parochial ministry as both experienced practitioner and theologian. He is married to Helen, a railway chaplain, and they have two adult children.